WORLD WITHOUT WANT

WORLD

WITHOUT

WANT

PAUL G. HOFFMAN

HARPER & ROW, PUBLISHERS

NEW YORK AND EVANSTON

I-N

LIBRARY OF CONGRESS CATALOG CARD NUMBER: 62-17087

CONTENTS

A PERSONAL WORD
TO THE READER

You and I are members of a privileged minority. The fact that we can read makes us members of that minority. If every one in the world capable of doing it were to read this book, we would *all* still be a minority.

More likely than not, you have had a good meal within the last few hours, live in a home with heat and light, wear adequate clothing, expect to live to watch your children become adults, expect your grandchildren to remember you. If you enjoy any one of these advantages, you are part of a small minority. If you expect to enjoy them all, you are among the favored few of this earth, and this book is written for you.

But it is not about you; it is about the majority. It deals with the 1.3 billion people living in less-developed countries and territories associated with the United Nations and for whom lives of decency and dignity have only recently become a hope. These people will not submit much longer to their ancient ways of life. They will not be satisfied with promises of progress. One way or another they will try to achieve quickly at least a little of what you and I already enjoy.

I hope I can convey to you in this book some sense of the seething unrest among people in the scores of under-developed countries I have visited in the last few years, some hint of the intensity of the people's determination to better their conditions, and some idea of their understand-able impatience, an impatience which is one of the most potent forces in the world today.

Their titanic struggle could lead to violence and war. It could produce other Congos, other Cubas—indeed, it could plunge the whole world into chaos.

This need not be; but we cannot sit by and do nothing. The pressure of demand today is so great that we cannot wait for the slow development which was characteristic of most of the industrially advanced nations. Processes that took centuries for us must be compressed into decades for the underdeveloped world.

Such progress is possible. There are available in almost all the underdeveloped countries the human and physical resources which, if effectively used, would assure better lives. The overwhelming share of responsibility for the economic and social progress of any country rests with the people of that country—but they must have our help.

And there are tremendous new allies on our side in the struggle. Science and technology have given men exciting new tools with which to improve their lives, just as they have opened up new pathways to the stars. Our knowledge and our aspirations have brought within reach the capacity to create, in freedom, a world without want.

PAUL G. HOFFMAN

WORLD WITHOUT WANT

1

THE FOUR HORSEMEN
OF OUR TIME

WALK DOWN the main street of Kasai village in the Congo. Look at the gaunt frames of the men and women—the swollen bellies of the children. This is hunger —with starvation just a yard's length away. Look at their eyes. As they meet yours, a glimmer of hope springs up. They cannot believe that you can see their plight and do nothing about it.

Duck your head and go into a small, dark hut in Nicaragua. There will be people, plenty of them, of all ages; but the darkness of their windowless home is as nothing compared to the darkness of their minds. Only one in every five Nicaraguan villagers can read or write.

Pause by the waterhole serving an Indonesian township. Who are these ghost figures barely able to lift their pitchers of water from the well? Some 96,000 people live in this area. A recent check revealed they all had malaria to a greater or lesser degree. Some of the people can work some of the time.

11

Two out of every three people alive today eke out a marginal existence struggling against the four malignant curses of our times: hunger, poverty, ignorance, and chronic ill health. For two billion of the world's three billion people, these spectral horsemen pervade the environment of daily life.

The Indian peasant is typical. He lives in a mud hut. He has few contacts beyond the next village; few roads exist, and when they do, they are usually miserable cart tracks over difficult terrain. If he is lucky, he has land— nearly 40 per cent of India's 330 million rural population do not. His pitiful holding may be in two or three or perhaps six widely separated plots. It is some of the most unproductive cultivated land in the world. The peasant cannot afford fertilizer, better seed, power machinery, or any but the most primitive farm tools. The annual income from the land for his family of six will be about $200, of which a third will be owed to a money lender. He will pour his energies into this land and get back from it barely enough for his family to eat.

He Sleeps on the Raw Earth

In other respects, his life is harsher still. For a bed he uses a straw pallet—or perhaps the raw earth. For fuel with which to cook his meager meals, he uses dried cow dung. The water he drinks is carried by his wife or children from a village well of doubtful purity. All the clothes he owns, he wears.

He can neither read nor write, and it is only recently that his children have been given the hope of learning. Malnutrition and illness are rife about him. If he gets sick, there is no doctor. He and his wife can expect that half their children will be dead before reaching the age of six. Any member of his family can consider himself fortunate if he lives to be forty years old.

Seventy-five per cent of India's 440 million people share this lot. Gandhi described the Indian peasant's life as an "eternal compulsory fast." These Indian peasants constitute 20 per cent of the agricultural and rural people—one out of every five—in the entire world.

City dwellers of the underdeveloped world fare little better. Thousands of them sleep in the streets, in winter and summer, huddling together or against a warm wall when the weather is cold. Epidemics run rampant.

In June 1961, *Life* magazine published a photographic essay on a slum family of Rio de Janeiro, Brazil, the Da Silva family. It was a revelation of unutterable squalor.

The father had come to the city to escape the burdens of peasant life. "Now he sells kerosene and bleach," *Life* said, "in a tiny boxlike stall which he and Nair (his wife) built—as they did their tiny shack—from tin cans, broken orange crates and stolen pieces of lumber. The shop brings in about $20 a month. To get $5 more to buy food, Nair, about to have her ninth child, washes clothes in the only available water—from a spigot at the foot of the hill. The children, who range from 12 years to 17 months, are penned in the shack or roam the foul pathways of the favela where the filth of the inhabitants is tossed out to rot." Both parents were unceasingly exhausted. None of the children had ever been as far as minutes away from his wretched hovel. They had no hope. The brutal drudgery of their lives had pounded the entire family into a mold of defeat from which there was no prospect of escape.

The care of the younger children was in the hands of twelve-year-old Flavio, one bright spot in the otherwise unrelieved gloom. But Flavio was sick and it seemed unlikely that he would get treatment in time to save his life.

HELP COMES—IN A FLOOD

United States readers' reaction to the story was immediate and generous. Almost overnight, the lives of Flavio and the rest of the Da Silva family were transformed. With contributions which flowed in from readers, a decent home was bought near schools for the children and near a clinic in which Nair could have her baby. The father was provided with a used truck to set him up in the delivery business. A hospital in Denver offered to care for Flavio for two years without charge, and he was flown there for treatment. In a year, he had grown three and one-quarter inches. A trust fund was set up for him. And there still was money enough left over to help the twenty thousand other residents of the favela build a primitive sewage-disposal system, some steps up the hillside, and the beginnings of a water system.

The tragedy of the underdeveloped world is that the story is not unusual, except for its happy ending. The Da Silva family is typical. They were no more poverty-stricken than their neighbors. And their slum existence is duplicated not by dozens or hundreds or thousands but, with minor differences, by dozens of millions all over the underdeveloped world.

The immediate hopes and expectations of the average man in this part of the world are simple enough. They include such things as a chance for his children to learn to read and write, a source of pure water, a reliable plow, a sewing machine, shoes, and two cooking pots instead of one. They include a doctor when he or his family needs one, enough food for tomorrow's meals as well as today's, seed with a slightly higher yield, perhaps a bicycle. They certainly include some protection for himself and his family when he is caught up in a natural disaster such as a drought or an insect plague or a delay in the life-giving monsoon rains.

This is not pie in the sky. In the developed nations many of these benefits are readily available, and the others can be obtained by a few hours of labor. But they are not yet within reach of the average man of the under-developed world.

He stands alone. He wrings subsistence from his environment with his bare hands. The dangers to his precarious existence are so clear, so present, and so far beyond his control that he can only try to ward them off by whatever magic seems to work. When the magic fails, a minor breakdown speedily becomes a disaster which he may or may not survive.

2

AN AWAKENING WORLD

It is only in the last few moments of time, as human history is recorded, that science and technology have created the means to wipe out the poverty, hunger, illiteracy, and chronic ill health that have been man's intimate companions. Yet the realization that a better life is possible has already spread to the far corners of the earth, bringing with it an awakening of explosive dimensions—a "revolution of rising expectations."

To suffer through a famine when no relief is available is one thing. To go hungry and see your children go hungry when you know food is within reach is quite another.

To watch your children grow up shackled by ignorance, when the written word is unavailable anyway, is one thing. To see your children permanently in bondage to illiteracy, when you know that escape should be possible, is entirely different.

To see your wife waste away with disease when there is no cure, and no doctor to administer it, is one thing. To watch the same tragedy when you know that the cure

Drought reduced this village in East Pakistan to famine. The woman at the right pours a drop of the precious water supply.

Distended belly, skinny limbs, great weakness are symptoms of *kwashiorkor,* one kind of malnutrition. This child in Tanganyika is only too typical of millions in the less-developed countries. Properly fed— perhaps by substituting protein for a high-starch diet—he can be on his way back to health in a matter of days.

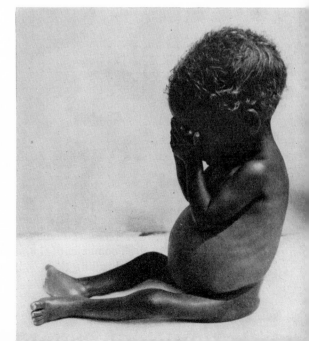

At night, the streets are home for scores of millions of people in one hundred countries of the world. These Bombay children rise at dawn and roll up their beds to clear way for pedestrians.

exists and the doctor is just out of reach is quite another story.

The Indian peasant and the Brazilian slum dweller know they could have a better life. Their counterparts in one hundred countries and territories—in two-thirds of the world—know it too. Yesterday, relief from grinding poverty was for them a distant dream. Today, it is a practical possibility. The ferment caused by this fact is perhaps the most important motive force of our time.

THE RICH AWAKEN TOO

The industrially advanced nations are also undergoing a process of awakening. We are learning to pay attention to the demands of the rest of the world—in our own interest. For if the yearnings of thousands of millions of people for a better life are not realized, the future promises one explosive outbreak after another.

Responsibility for the headlong plunge that the backward nations wish to take into the twentieth century is primarily theirs, but they need help. If, through their own efforts plus the needed external assistance, these people do achieve better lives, the world may become a safer and happier place than anyone has dared to hope. More than any other single factor, the response to these demands is determining the political and social complexion of the future.

We are in the second decade of an organized response to the needs of the less-developed areas, of those nations which are attempting to modernize. Yet some among us still are inclined to ask why we should be concerned. The high standard of living we enjoy was achieved through hard work and through the application of our technical and business talents, they say. Why shouldn't we leave to the peoples of the less-developed countries the solving of their own development problems?

One answer is that foreign aid in the form of both capital and technicians contributed greatly to the growth of the United States in its early years. British capital, for example, built several of the first American railroads. Another answer is that our political and business future is so inextricably bound up with theirs that our own interests compel involvement.

GOOD BUSINESS

In the long view, the one hundred underdeveloped countries are a great new economic frontier. If per capita incomes in the underdeveloped world were to be lifted in the 1960s, steadily year by year, by only 2.5 per cent, exports to these countries from the industrially advanced world, which totaled $164 billion for the ten years 1950–1960, should reach $350 billion for 1960–1970. For the United States—assuming it retains its current share of the international trade flow—such an increase would mean, by 1970, an estimated additional $8.5 billion in exports every year.

An equivalent of more than 4.5 million jobs in the United States now depend on foreign trade. Of these, more than 1.75 million jobs depend on United States exports to the underdeveloped areas of the world. By 1970 this number could well increase to the equivalent of more than 2.75 million full-time jobs.

That is good business. Foreign aid is not charity; it is sound business management in the same sense as the more familiar forms of product or market development.

It is also a major contribution to political stability. After

World War II the long-smothered feelings of national-ism in the underdeveloped areas found expression as nation after nation demanded and achieved independence. Fifty-one nations constituted the original signatories to the UN charter in 1945. By 1962, the UN had more than one hundred members; and of the new members, over thirty had attained their independence or were created after 1945.

The leaders of many if not most of these nations are moderates. They know that progress, to be enduring, must come by evolution and not by violence. But their peoples are impatient. Visible signs of improvement are urgently needed. These poverty-stricken people want schools for their children, doctors for themselves and their families, a chance to earn a decent livelihood—and they want all these things now.

Massive propaganda is aimed at convincing them that progress toward these goals can come only through violent revolution. To combat this pressure, their leaders must show results. Regardless of how dedicated the leaders may be or how industrious the people, satisfactory results can be achieved only as external aid is made available to speed up the evolutionary process. Foreign aid is, therefore, an investment in a more peaceful world for ourselves and our children.

"If we grasp this opportunity to build an age of productive partnership between the less fortunate nations and those that have already achieved a high state of economic advancement," former President Eisenhower has said, "we will make brighter the outlook for a world order based upon security, freedom, and peace. Otherwise, the outlook could be dark indeed. We face what could be a turning point in history, and we must act decisively."

CALL FOR ACTION

President Kennedy has urged action through the United Nations. "My nation, which has freely shared its capital and its technology to help others help themselves, now proposes officially designating this decade of the 1960s as the UN Decade of Development," he said in the UN General Assembly in 1961. "Under the framework of that resolution, the UN's existing efforts in promoting economic growth can be expanded and coordinated. . . . Development can become a cooperative, not a competitive enterprise—to enable all nations, however diverse in their systems and beliefs, to become in fact as well as in law free and equal states."

Perhaps the strongest of all reasons for assisting under-privileged peoples is the one given by General Charles de Gaulle, who said, "It is the duty of those who are best endowed and strongest to help others—those who are in want, those who are underprivileged. This they must do if they themselves do not want to perish."

Secretary-General U Thant has put it this way:

Can our imagination match our abundance only when the ugly, destructive risks of war are at work? Is the only challenge we recognize the challenge of fear—in weapons, in outer space, in international rivalry? Is there no way in which the great constructive and peaceful purposes of man can so grip our heart and conscience that the spending needed to end starvation, to prevent the death of little children, to shelter the homeless and clothe the naked come to have first priority in the purposes of the human race?

The doctrines of every major religion require the rich to act compassionately toward the poor. And if moral codes fail to command positive action, the negative whip of an uneasy and inescapable conscience compels our attention to the needs of stricken people.

Morally we cannot escape concern; politically the seething unrest demands it; economically, we will gain from it. The bluntest and most accurate answer to why we should be concerned is that we must be, if we are to survive.

3

FACT AND FABLE

A WORLDWIDE ATTACK on poverty cannot be fully effective until certain persistent myths are disposed of. One is the theory of the "happy native."

We are told by its proponents that the peasant cultivator lives an idyllic life close to the bosom of mother earth. His wants and needs are simple. He is happy. Indeed, we are told, it is we who are unhappy; our goal should be to emulate the simple dignity of the man in the fields.

Of course the advocates of this romantic view know the peasant cultivator only from the pages of a colorfully illustrated travel magazine or from a brief glimpse through the windows of an air-conditioned railroad car. Their noses have not been rubbed in the grime and misery of the peasant's daily life. They have never had to work to exhaustion day after day for the equivalent of half a loaf of bread.

No, the happy native exists almost solely in conversations at cocktail parties in well-appointed living rooms. A recent investigation disclosed that there are as many

24

stomach ulcers (which are reputed to be induced partly by tension) per one thousand persons in Indonesia as in New York.

Another myth is that "natives" are "stubborn" and will not be helped. This myth takes many forms, and affects the thinking of many people.

MISGUIDED HELP

In an isolated primitive village in Central America, women prepare the evening meal for their families on a makeshift stove which lies flat on the floor. The position and construction of the stove requires the women to stoop, bend, and squat.

A community worker, observing this apparently needless waste of energy, evolved a plan for an inexpensive upright oven. It was quickly and eagerly adopted by the women of the village; but a few months later, when the community worker returned to the village, she was amazed to discover the flat stoves back in operation and the upright ovens abandoned.

It took her a while to discover why the women of the village apparently preferred the extra work. The new oven had disrupted the pattern of life in the village. The men and children had been in the habit of lingering around the stove in the evening after eating. The new oven, placed differently, was not suitable to this informal arrangement. The men were slipping out in the evening and congregating in the equivalent of a village pub—so the women decided the new ovens were expendable.

In a Turkish experiment, UN technicians demonstrated that removing the rocks from the field made plowing and cultivation much easier. But the crops failed, and it was later discovered that the rocks held moisture in the ground over a prolonged and regular dry season. The local people who refused to remove the rocks—stubborn though they were—were right.

Many times, of course, the shoe is on the other foot. The "natives" are wrong. But people in underdeveloped countries, conservative though they are—indeed, frightened as they are of change which might destroy their marginal livelihood—are willing to adopt proven new methods.

Fishermen in a Ceylonese village watched a Food and Agriculture Organization demonstration for several weeks. They saw men go out in the same boats as their own, but with the addition of an outboard motor. Then they watched catches being brought in which were double and triple their own. There was no resistance to outboard motors after that. The "stubborn native" simply wants proof.

MYTH ABOUT "SUPERIORITY"

There is a pernicious myth that lighter-skinned peoples who predominate in industrialized countries are superior to people with colored skin. Many still believe, despite evidence to the contrary, that the darker-skinned peoples are incapable of absorbing the education, of acquiring the skills, and of exercising the judgment needed for economic development.

With some who believe in this myth, there is no use presenting evidence or discussing the question. But with others, whose only guilt is an unthinking acceptance of inherited misconceptions, a simple look at the leaders of much of Asia, Africa, and Latin America and at what

United Nations

A donkey-drawn cart stands in sharp contrast to the locomotive in this coastal area of Colombia, a country in the second stage of development.

India is ready for economic take-off. Improvement of transport, especially of major ports and railways, has been given the highest priority. With the help of a World Bank loan, the port capacity of Calcutta is being expanded to enable it to handle eleven million tons of traffic annually.

United Nations

United Nations

Because tools are expensive and manpower abundant, this dam on the Bhadra River in India is built almost entirely by hand. Granite stones and rocks are first stacked in dumps; from there they are transported close to the dam; and then teams of men carry them on bamboo poles to the work site. Boulders weighing up to 1½ tons are transported this way. Women carry the mortar to the site in shallow iron bowls balanced on their heads.

the peoples of such areas as India, Mexico, and Puerto Rico have already accomplished in an amazingly short time is enough to destroy these attitudes.

Any close look at the peoples of underdeveloped nations will reveal that the human race is made up of about the same cross section of types in every country. Intelligence, capacity, ability, and even poverty know no color line.

MYTHS ABOUT COLONIALISM

Another myth—or rather system of myths—concerns colonialism. On the one hand, many of the citizens of former colony-owning countries feel that they made a substantial contribution to the welfare and development of their former colonies. On the other hand, deep-seated resentments in the former colonies blind the citizens to everything but the memory of exploitation. Both points of view are emotionally charged, and the peoples of both groups are extremely sensitive on the subject.

An objective look at colonialism shows that the truth is somewhere in between. Colonialism, in many of its forms, was exploitative and often ugly. But the colonial powers frequently made substantial contributions to health and education, and in many instances injected the first industrial capital into the underdeveloped lands—the roads, docks, mining equipment, railroads, and other appurtenances of industrialization. In some instances, they brought another prerequisite of development: stable government. And they certainly brought to the peoples of the colonial areas an awareness of the possibilities of material improvement.

To assign colonialism the full blame for underdevelopment is unfair. In some cases it held development back, but in others it should be credited with the first few steps forward.

Parallel with the myth about colonialism is another myth: that independence, in and of itself, guarantees development. History contradicts this belief. Some long-independent countries are among the least developed, and independence can, at the beginning, add to the problems of development. On the other hand, when the initial handicaps are overcome, independence does provide an incentive for sharply accelerated development.

MYTHS ABOUT GEOGRAPHY

There is a myth about climate. Many of the under-developed countries lie in tropical and semitropical areas. Can their poverty be traced simply to the heat?

Not many years ago the climatic explanation of economic backwardness was widely accepted. The tropics, it was said, made men lazy; more charitably, it was stated that hard and sustained labor was impossible in the equatorial and near-equatorial zones.

Today, however, one must be chary of ascribing under-development to the influence of climate. To be sure, there are parts of the world where the heat is debilitating, but such locales are the exception rather than the rule. Even when the heat is fierce, it sometimes occurs only during a few hours of the day or months of the year. In addition, some tropical areas, such as the Queensland region of Australia, have shown vigorous economic growth.

Moreover, the underdeveloped countries are not all tropical. Korea has a temperate climate, as does much of

highland Africa, Argentina, and Chile. It has been
pointed out that there is no significant difference in attitudes or productivity between Indonesians living at sea
level and those living in the invigorating climate four
thousand feet up in the mountains.

Other investigators into the relationship between climate and economic backwardness have concerned themselves with rainfall. Much of the problem of the African
continent revolves around its unevenly distributed pre-
cipitation and the inability of its inhabitants to control
and utilize water. Along the great northern strip of Africa,
the Arab peoples have for centuries contended with a rainfall that is sporadic and insufficient, while large areas of
tropical Africa alternately wash away under torrential
downpours or parch under none. Asians, too, have had to
live with unfavorable distribution of annual rainfall. The
monsoons call the tune for all of South Asian agriculture,
and when they are late, the crops die in the fields. Yet
South America as a whole has no such problem, and it is
largely underdeveloped. In another era, North Africa—
better tilled, irrigated, and tended than today—helped
feed Caesar's Legions.

As with climate, the pattern of rainfall provides at best
only a partial explanation for underdevelopment. More
important, neither heat nor rainfall seems to pose insuperable obstacles to development. Air conditioning, water
storage, and irrigation can go a long way toward improving the physical environment in these respects—as witness
the economic progress of both Australia and Israel or,
for that matter, Arizona, Kansas (once called the Great
American Desert), and California.

The peoples of the tropics and the deserts will always
have to reckon with and adapt to geographic liabilities,

but these need not keep most such regions from eventually joining the ranks of the more prosperous nations of the world.

MYTHS ABOUT COSTS

One of the most prevalent myths about development concerns its cost for the industrialized nations. Because budget makers and legislators find it convenient to describe these costs in terms solely of dollars or other currencies, we have come to think that these costs simply represent outpourings of cash—dollar bills—which in turn are extracted from the taxpayer's wallet.

This is not true. What the underdeveloped nations want and need—and what we have given them and will give them in large part in the future—is goods and technical services. True, these things must be paid for with money, but far less money comes from the taxpayer's pocket than the figures would indicate. Some "foreign aid" is, in effect, a subsidy for a country's exports. Goods sent to the underdeveloped countries mean jobs for workers in the industrialized nations. They mean greater profits through increased trade. They mean absorption of surplus commodities with a consequent firming of prices. They mean that, because of economic expansion, more taxes can be collected without a corresponding rise in tax rates.

In short, the betterment of business that results from aid to the underdeveloped countries serves to make the actual out-of-pocket cost of such a program substantially less than its book cost.

4

WHAT IS AN UNDERDEVELOPED
COUNTRY?

An underdeveloped country is not simply a poverty-stricken version of a developed nation. It is a country
which lacks the means to eradicate its own poverty. The
roads and railroads are insufficient, the communication
system is erratic, the factories and the tools for agriculture
are mostly lacking. Few people have enough education
and training to take part usefully in the development
process. In twenty countries today, only 5 per cent of the
population can read or write; in one hundred others,
literacy is below the 50 per cent mark. Hospitals and other
medical services are pitifully inadequate, with perhaps
one doctor for every ten thousand or twenty thousand
people.

Whatever wealth underdeveloped countries have is
often concentrated in the hands of a few people who live
in comparative opulence surrounded by overwhelming
poverty. An underdeveloped country's banking system is
embryonic; small loans have to be obtained through

money lenders who are often little better than extortionists. Not only are there scant savings from which investment could be made, but the people who have wealth usually refuse to invest it productively in their own countries.

The underdeveloped nation's exports typically consist almost entirely of raw materials, ores, fruits, or some other staple product with perhaps a small admixture of handicrafts or luxury goods. Often extraction or production of these export commodities is wholly or partly under foreign control, with little of the profit being reinvested in the country.

YARDSTICKS SOUGHT

But while it is easy to recognize a country that is under-developed, it is extremely difficult to set up an exact statistical definition of what constitutes underdevelopment. Over the last fifty years or so, industrial nations such as the United States and many countries in Western Europe have been carefully watching and measuring their own economies with a variety of statistical yardsticks. For example, the United States knows with considerable precision how much money its banks lent last month, how many freight cars were loaded, how much money was paid out in wages and at what rates, and how many people were employed. The underdeveloped country, lacking many reliable business and government statistics, cannot measure its own economy in this way. It has some figures and can guess at others, but by and large it lacks information about itself. In most parts of Africa, for instance, it is virtually impossible to get accurate figures on the population because there is no uniform system, if there is any system at all, for registering births and deaths in the jungles and villages.

This ignorance is a barrier to progress. It is not enough to know in general that one's problems are huge. In order to tackle them intelligently, governments need to know their exact dimensions. As has been said, "If you don't get the facts, the facts will get you."

International organizations have done a great deal to push back the fog of statistical darkness. One important United Nations task is to help underdeveloped nations set up fact-finding services. The UN then correlates and coordinates the available statistics for the whole world.

Out of these efforts a general picture is beginning to emerge. Where detailed statistics are lacking, generalizations can be made based on samples, and projections can be drawn from known trends.

Using such statistics as are available, one can arrive at a rough general definition of an underdeveloped country and get some idea of the number of such countries and the extent of their economic problems, even though we must admit that any such generalizations are somewhat arbitrary.

Income as a Yardstick

One of the simplest yardsticks for measuring a country's relative development is the average annual per capita income of its citizens. This index is reached by taking a country's total income, as revealed through production figures and other data, and dividing it by the number of persons in the country of whatever age or condition. This average is then stated in terms of a common currency such as United States dollars.

Admittedly, this index does not express the actual income of any one person or group. Moreover, averages tend to hide extremes, especially when the extremes are great. In a small country where most citizens are very poor, the incomes of a few millionaires will raise the average substantially. In addition, the same per capita income may have different significance in different countries. Where food is cheap or needs for clothing and shelter are minimal, a low income is more tolerable than in a land where food is scarce and costly, or where cold winters make heavy clothing and warm houses necessities for everyone.

National and per capita income figures for underdeveloped countries are, therefore, only informed estimates. Moreover, to state the income figures in dollars per year, it is necessary to convert local income statistics into dollars—and generally at the official rate of exchange. The official dollar rate of exchange is often an inadequate way of measuring the local purchasing power of *pesos* or *rupees* or *rials*. One can buy a good deal more rice in Thailand for one *baht* than could be purchased at an American supermarket for five cents, which is the equivalent in United States currency at the official exchange rate. In addition, this method of translating local per capita income into dollars understates the real income level of low-income countries because it cannot take into account the pattern of local life and the fact that many necessities are produced at home or bartered in the villages and thus do not enter fully into national-income statistics.

Nevertheless, income figures do provide a useful and, within limits, a reliable way of measuring a country's state of development. In a few of the one hundred underdeveloped countries and territories with which the United

Nations is concerned, the average annual per capita income is as high as $700. In four-fifths of the underdeveloped countries, annual per capita income is well below $300, and in half of these countries the average is less than $100 per person per year—or less than many people in the industrially advanced world would expect to earn in a week.

RUNGS ON THE LADDER

Underdeveloped countries fall roughly into three groups. Walt Rostow, in his study of *The Stages of Economic Growth** calls them the "traditional society," the "pre-condition stage," and the "take-off" stage. Actually, these categories are far from rigid; the dividing line between countries in the "pre-condition" and "take-off" stages is especially difficult to distinguish.

The Republic of Togo, a newly independent country on the west coast of Africa, is a possible example of a "traditional society." Primitive and tribal, its people have had little contact with the outside world. Prior to independence in 1960, there was no tax system worthy of the name. There were few roads, few schools, few trained leaders, few banks, few houses. The annual per capita income of its nearly 1.5 million people was well below $100. Food production, education, government service, trade— virtually everything was tragically inadequate.

With aid from the United Nations and other sources, particularly France, President Sylvanus Olympio has begun to weld the people into a national unit. He has started them on the road to a better tomorrow. There is a long way to go, but Togo has begun.

* London: Cambridge University Press, 1960.

TABLE 1

THE UNDERDEVELOPED AREAS

Countries and Territories—Grouped According to Per Capita Income, Annual Average 1957–1959

(1960 population in thousands)[1]

Under $100		Under $100	
Country	*Population*	*Country*	*Population*
Afghanistan	13,800	Mali	4,100
Albania	1,607	Mauritania	727
Angola (Port.)	4,605	Martinique (Fr.)	277
Basutoland (UK)	685	Mozambique (Port.)	6,385
Bechuanaland (UK)	340	Nepal	9,180
Bolivia	3,462	Netherlands (New Guinea)	735
Burma	20,662	New Guinea (Aust. admin.)	1,402
Cambodia	4,952	Niger	2,870
Cameroon	4,097	Pakistan	92,727
Central African Republic	1,227	Papua (Aust.)	503
Chad	2,639	Portuguese Guinea	571
China[2]	10,612	Portuguese Timor	502
Congo (Leopoldville)	14,150	Reunion (Fr.)	336
Dahomey	1,934	Ruanda-Urundi (Belg.)	4,901
Ethiopia	20,000	Sierra Leone	2,450
Federation of Nigeria	35,091	Somalia	1,990
Gambia (UK)	284	South West Africa (So. Afr.)	522
Guadeloupe and dep. (Fr.)	270	Spanish Guinea	246
Guinea	3,000	Sudan	11,770
Haiti	3,505	Swaziland (UK)	259
India	432,567	Tanganyika	9,239
Indonesia	92,600	Thailand	25,520
Jordan	1,695	Togo	1,440
Kenya (UK)	7,131	Uganda (UK)	6,677
Laos	1,805	Yemen	5,000
Liberia	1,290	Upper Volta	3,635

[1] Source of population figures: *1961 United Nations Statistical Yearbook.*
[2] Reliable figures not available for Mainland China, North Korea, North Viet-Nam. Source of income figures: United Nations Statistical Office.

TABLE 1 (Continued)

$100–$199			$200–$299	
Country	Population		Country	Population
Brazil	65,743		British Guiana	567
Ceylon	9,896		Bulgaria	7,867
Congo (Brazzaville)	795		Colombia	14,132
Dominican Republic	2,994		Federation of Malaya	6,909
Ecuador	4,317		Fiji Islands (UK)	394
El Salvador	2,612		Greece	8,327
Gabon	440		Hong Kong (UK)	2,981
Ghana	6,691		Mauritius and dep. (UK)	639
Guatemala	3,765		Mexico	34,923
Honduras	1,883		Portugal	8,921
Iran	20,182		Romania	18,403
Iraq	7,085		Surinam (Neth.)	270
Ivory Coast	3,230		Yugoslavia	18,538
Korea, Republic of	24,665			

$300–$699	
Argentina	20,006
Chile	7,340
Costa Rica	1,171
Cuba	6,797
Cyprus	563
Hungary	9,999
Israel	2,114
Lebanon	1,646
Malta and Gozo (UK)	329
North Borneo (UK)	454
Panama	1,055
Poland	29,703
Puerto Rico (US)	2,361
Sarawak (UK)	745
Singapore (UK)	1,634
Spain	30,128
Uruguay	2,827
Venezuela	7,524
West Indies (UK)	3,115

$100–$199 (continued):

Country	Population
Libya	1,195
Madagascar	5,393
Morocco	11,626
Nicaragua	1,477
Paraguay	1,768
Peru	10,857
Philippines	27,500
Rhodesia and Nyasaland (UK)	8,330
Ryukyu Islands (US)	883
Saudi Arabia	6,036
Senegal	2,973
Tunisia	4,168
Turkey	27,561
United Arab Republic	25,929
Viet-Nam, Republic of	14,100
Zanzibar and Pemba (UK)	307

$200–$299

Country	Population
Algeria (Fr.)	11,020
Bhutan (Indian admin.)	670

A country in the "pre-conditions" stage is Colombia. Indeed, Colombia may be a bit past this arduous stage. It is a country of more than fourteen million people, with an annual per capita income of about $250. With UN help, it is actively spurring such things as social security, government administration, warehouse management, land reform, inland fisheries, leprosy control, and teacher training. It is studying its soil so as to put it to better use and is encouraging small industries. Colombia is still largely agricultural, but diversified industry is under way.

India is nearing the "take-off" stage. Just when it will become self-propelling is something on which experts disagree; some put the date as early as 1971, others as late as 1980. Prime Minister Jawaharlal Nehru estimates 1972 or 1973.

India's 440 million people make an average of only $65 per person per year, and their problems are tremendous. India is hampered by primitive agricultural patterns, poor tools, tiny farms, and rural inertia. Many of her people are near starvation. But industry is making good progress, and agriculture as well. Her resources—in coal, iron ore, manganese, titanium and mica—include the elements needed not only for basic industries but also for chemical, atomic energy, and other of the more advanced technologies.

India also has a plan and a program. It requires $1 billion per year of investment and assistance from outside sources. India's own people—who exist on an average of eighteen cents in income per day—are putting up the remaining $3 billion a year needed to carry it out.

If the outside investment is forthcoming and if the plan succeeds (as there is every indication that it will), India will be well on the way to joining the family of free industrial nations and will in turn be capable of making more significant contributions to the conquest of poverty in other parts of the world. She has a stable government, a good civil service, and a people dedicated to modernization. One day, her own savings and export earnings will pay for the tools and raw materials she must import, and for the payment of her debts. This is what is meant by "take-off." At that point, the "eternal compulsory fast" would begin to come to an end.

5

BREAKING THE CHAINS
OF CUSTOM

In some low-income countries, physical labor is considered beneath the dignity of men. Hunting, fishing, fighting, and politicking are the only respectable occupations. Work in the home, in the fields, and in the markets is, normally for women, and women only.

This is one of a number of severe obstacles to economic growth arising from deep-seated mental attitudes which time and tradition have produced. Breaking through these obstacles is a tremendous jolt when it happens for the first time.

Getting men to go to work is just the beginning. In many countries where they are willing to work, they will perform only certain tasks. The people who enjoy prestige in these countries are government employees, lawyers, doctors, and priests—so everyone wants to hold one of these jobs. Men engaged in business and trade are looked upon as third-class citizens—and the country suffers. It needs such men.

Denial of equal rights to women is also an obstacle to economic development. It is surprising, perhaps, but true that there is a close relationship between the way women are treated in a country and the progress that country has made toward a good life. Where women are virtual slaves, forbidden so much as to go out of the house without their husbands, given no rights whatever in society, the country is invariably primitive. Where women have been largely emancipated, as in Japan, tremendous strides are being made toward modernization.

The reasons are clear. When a country keeps its women in bondage, half its available brain power is lost. Moreover, the children—boys as well as girls—are brought up under the guidance of an ignorant mother.

In some countries it actually is considered pointless to educate the girl child. "If you teach her to write, she will start writing love letters." So schools, especially in rural sections, are filled with boys. These countries are finding their economic development slow and painful.

IGNORANCE AND HABIT

Taboos and superstitions also stand in the way of progress. The women in one African village refused to let the United Nations pipe in pure water. The water they carried laboriously in gourds from a mudhole was unfit to drink, but they insisted on using it because, they said, it gave them fertility.

In parts of Africa, witch doctors and fetish priests retain a powerful hold on the people and do their wily best to frustrate change. They refuse to let in medicines, lest faith in their own methods be undermined. A group of policemen in an African country arrested a UN weather expert and threw him into prison. When asked why, the local police pointed to balloons which the weather man had been sending aloft and said he was trying to steal their climate so as to sell it to their enemies. The UN aide gained his freedom by persuading the police that he was a very inefficient thief: the balloons were too small to have done much damage.

Patience and understanding, combined with intelligent compassion, will be required in such areas. There are deep-rooted reasons for many of these attitudes. They will not be changed easily.

In the first place, the vast majority—70 per cent to 80 per cent—of the peoples of Africa, Asia, and Latin America are peasants. "Peasant" is not another word for farmer. A successful farmer in industrialized countries is a businessman of the land. He is progressive and forward looking. The peasant, on the other hand, is extremely conservative. He is fearful of change.

No Margin for Error

As we have seen, the theory that he is by nature mulish, obstinate, or stupid is a myth, but he is operating in a world in which there is no margin for error, no room for maneuvering. He knows the practices of the past that have worked for his ancestors and for him. Yet the peasant will change his ways once it has been demonstrated that he will benefit by so doing. Peasants in Afghanistan, for example, were afraid to use the pulp of the sugar-beet plant—which they had in abundance—to feed their hungry livestock. They thought it would make them sick. United Nations people brought in some cattle, fed the pulp to them, and showed how the cattle thrived. Thereafter the

FAO—Studios du Souissi, Rabat

Symbolic of man's struggle against natural disaster throughout the ages is this locust invasion of Morocco, being combated with poison bait.

orange tree af-
the locusts have
sed.

FAO—Studios du Souissi, Rabat

WHO—Paul Almasy

Three times a week, drinking water comes to this suburb of 25,000 inhabitants in Peru. At variable pressure, it flows for about three hours in the morning from three small pipes. The queue forms early; first come, first served.

With United Nations assistance, the government of West Bengal takes major steps to provide a more adequate water supply system for the five million inhabitants of Greater Calcutta. At present the daily supply is short by some fifty million gallons.

WHO—Paul Almasy

peasants readily followed suit—and both the cattle and the peasants benefited.

Like the peasant, the city worker in the underdeveloped countries is not easily transformed into a member of a modern society. He is generally unskilled and must be trained for some of the simplest of tasks. Nevertheless, despite the obstacles, significant progress is being made in developing efficient workers in many of the low-income countries. Some of these workers are proving to be the most teachable people in the world.

The attitude of wealthy people can be a serious block to development. Some use their wealth constructively. But too many of them are callous to the conditions in which the majority live. Instead of investing their wealth within their own country, they invest it abroad or store it in foreign banks. They block land reform, evade taxes, and flaunt their luxury before their underfed countrymen.

In such situations tax reform is essential. Such reform, however, must not destroy the incentive for private risk. And strictly honest systems of tax collection are vitally important.

All the people—not merely the wealthy—need incentives. In too many countries the shops are nearly bare; the materials for building a better home are nonexistent; there are no teachers to teach the children; pots and pans and stoves are not available. People will intensify their efforts when attractive, reasonably-priced consumer goods can be purchased. They turn out and build their own schools when the government helps them get teachers.

Nor are material incentives enough by themselves. There must be increasing opportunities, particularly for young people. In the underdeveloped world, people often feel unable to participate in improvement. Successful

leadership transforms wishful thinking into sound op-
timism—and effort. The sense of dedication which is vital
for successful development must be stirred. Mahatma
Gandhi personally spun thread and lived with the un-
touchables to fire their enthusiasm.

THE COIN HAS TWO SIDES

The attitudes that hamper development are not found
exclusively in underdeveloped countries. A European engineer, sent to advise in the construction of a hydroelectric dam in an Asian country, was shocked to see thousands of men and women carrying earth on their heads to
the dam site. He could not understand why responsible local engineers had not asked for modern earth-moving
equipment. He did not comprehend that construction of
the dam was temporarily robbing thousands of local inhabitants of their livelihood by tearing up their land, and
that earth-carrying was producing family income to tide
the people over while their lives were disrupted.

We of the industrialized countries have trouble re-
sponding to needs different from our own. "You scratch
us where it doesn't itch," one Latin peasant complained.
Many vaunted scientific and technological skills, which we
consider capable of virtually any miracles, have long since
bypassed the present needs of the African, Asian, and
Latin American.

We are concerned with labor-saving devices; they are
concerned with putting people to work productively. We
produce sugar substitutes and strain ourselves periodically
to diet away the caloric impact of the four-and-a-half
pounds of food we eat every day; they strain hard to get
and eat 1.2 pounds of food a day.

The productivity of a man is at least in part a result of the power he can add to his own muscles. But what economic use is it to a poor African if science harnesses a million pounds of thrust to shoot a rocket into orbit? What use is an electric can opener to an Asian? How often can a Latin American justify a wheat combine that can harvest a hundred acres a day?

Goals and methods must be worked out, not in terms of our sophisticated societies, but in terms of actual conditions in the underdeveloped countries. These goals must be attainable, the methods sensible and realistic. The psychological barriers to development are ours as well as theirs; the coin has two sides.

THE NEED FOR PLANNING

A severe obstacle to economic growth is the lack of adequate planning. In most of the underdeveloped countries, planning is haphazard at best. Slender resources too often have been devoted to glamor products such as ornate government buildings or wide boulevards in the capital rather than to schoolhouses and farm-to-market roads.

Yet it should be obvious that careful thought and preparation are necessary. Someone must decide whether the dam should come before the school and after the hospital, or whether the order should be reversed. This should be done by the highest authority in the country. The prime minister or president is the man most likely to put the national interest above factionalism, regionalism, or favoritism.

Unfortunately, the power of choice is frequently given to individual ministries or departments which champion their own pet projects. As a result, a shiny new factory in area "A" operates way below capacity because no provision has been made to move its product to the market in sector "B." A superhighway (a fine showpiece) is routed five hundred miles from the place where it is needed.

Some years ago, an elaborate steel rolling mill was built outside Rangoon, Burma, to make use of scrap iron left over from World War II. No one, however, had made an adequate survey of raw material requirements, or of the availability of trained managers and workers. The result was confusion, waste, and great disappointment. Finally, outside equipment and technicians were able to rescue the ill-prepared venture and a limited range of products is now being produced. Forward planning would have avoided these unnecessary and expensive growing pains.

Economic planning does not imply compulsion. It is not the same thing as a "planned economy." Free societies plan (though they may call it "programming" to fend off criticism). It amounts to nothing more nor less than intelligent thinking ahead—and it is essential to ensure orderly economic growth. The United Nations and its agencies are offering extensive help to countries just learning the technique.

6

THE MAGIC INGREDIENTS:
EDUCATION AND TRAINING

In July 1960, shortly after the Belgian Congo had gained its independence, a cruel confidence game was uncovered in Leopoldville. A man had gone about selling "college entrance certificates"—packets containing cards of admission to a fictional university, forged airplane tickets, and other "travel documents." At least scores of the packets had been sold for up to $50 each—a fabulous sum in the eyes of many who paid it out. When the hoax finally was uncovered, the discovery that they were not going to college after all caused the purchasers more frustration and fury than all the loss of their money.

There is, everywhere in the underdeveloped world, a tremendous hunger for learning. The people and their leaders know well that if they are to modernize, they must channel into economic development the "magic ingredients" of education and training. Waldemar Neilsen, president of the African-American Institute, said in March 1962, "This hunger, this belief in education is something

51

more powerful, more vivid, more real, more motivating than anyone can imagine who hasn't been there and hasn't seen it."

People voluntarily turn out in multitudes to erect school buildings. When a school opens to serve one area, children from nearby areas where no school is yet available will walk miles just to hang around the doorway, or sit on the window ledge, in hopes of overhearing a bit of the precious mystery which is happening in the class.

In tropical Africa alone, UNESCO estimates that about seventeen million children are without classroom space; between 80 per cent and 85 per cent of the adult population is illiterate; fewer than 5 per cent of the children who do attend primary school go on to secondary school; fewer than 1 per cent of those attending school are enrolled in vocational training institutes.

A five-year program has been adopted by the education ministers of this area which calls for a 77 per cent increase in primary school enrollment, a doubling of secondary school and university enrollment. To achieve even this modest goal at least 450,000 teachers must be trained.

THE WORLDWIDE PROBLEM

Taking the underdeveloped world as a whole, the picture becomes more staggering. Of the 1.3 billion persons in these one hundred countries and territories, some 750 million at or over school age cannot read or write.

And literacy alone is not enough. Scores of millions must be given secondary education as well. There are immense needs for vocational training, and vast numbers of people will need to qualify for highly skilled occupations. A conservative estimate for the immediate future shows a need to train one million people as top-level administrators, professional workers, executives, and middle-level technicians. The education and training task that lies ahead is truly formidable.

The hunger for education is so strong that some politicians have campaigned on platforms of quick universal free education. When these politicians get in power, they must deliver. But although primary education is the popular demand, it may prove wiser from a development point of view to spend the slender resources that are available on fewer people. Development can proceed more rapidly when part of the population is well educated than when all the population is partly educated. A well-trained cadre around which the beginnings of industrialization could be built would produce additional income, and hence additional tax money for education, perhaps leading to speedier universal primary education in the end. But no popularly elected political leader of the underdeveloped world would be likely to stay in office for long if he so much as wondered aloud whether expenditures for primary education might better be diverted to selective secondary schooling.

A short time ago the government of Nigeria—facing acute financial problems—sought to save money by closing a public primary school. Hundreds of people rioted. The school—and others previously scheduled for closing—had to remain open.

Education is more than a boon. It is an investment in human resources, perhaps the most important kind of investment we can make.

HUMAN CAPITAL VITAL

Theodore Schultz of the University of Chicago points out that:*

Perhaps the greatest capital formation that has been going on in our society is our investment in ourselves. It may be that these investments in ourselves—in our abilities, our talents and capacities, in our stamina, our health, the way we live and what we eat—are the very kinds of capital that make the greatest return in terms of reward for our efforts.

Frederick Harbison of Princeton University observes:†

A country's capacity to utilize effectively physical capital is dependent upon the availability of human capital, and vice versa. And it is essential for politicians and planners to understand that any development plan which does not give high priority to human-capital formation is simply unrealistic and almost certainly destined to fail, for experience has shown repeatedly that high-level manpower does not appear automatically or magically as dams, roads, factories, hospitals, radio stations, and airports come into existence.

All developing countries share a shortage of "high level manpower"—i.e., scientists, agronomists, veterinarians, engineers, teachers, doctors, government administrators, business leaders, and plant managers. The need for people at a middle level is even more crucial, not only because there are more jobs for people with middle-grade skills, but also because when they are not available, top-level professional people have to waste time doing their work. In West Africa, Asia, and Latin America, for example, graduate engineers may be found handling the

* "Human Wealth and Economic Growth," *The Humanist*, XIX, No. 2 (March–April 1959).
† *The Strategy of Human Resource Development in Modernizing Economies.*

FAO

The United Nations sent an expert to Ceylon to advise on improving the efficiency of its fishing fleet and gear. Six up-to-date boats, one of which is shown above, were imported from Denmark on his advice and their use was demonstrated. Now the Ceylonese fishermen are equipping their ancient catamarans with outboard motors.

When Libya became independent, a large UN mission was sent to assist in the development of its agriculture, forestry, and marketing. A leather specialist introduced new methods to prevent cuts in the skins, decay, and generally poor curing. Now cured hides and skins count among Libya's most important export items.

FAO

Clinton Rehling, UN Special Fund

A market in Togo. A nation in the first stages of development. it is still dependent in many ways upon traditional tribal organizations and institutions.

Refugees overflowing from China into Hong Kong epitomize many problems, including worldwide population growth.

The supply line for a campaign being mounted against malaria in the foothills of Nepal.

In India, elephants often are important members of malaria teams making their way into the depths of the forests through marshes and across lakes.

routine operation of an electric power sub-station or doing the work of draftsmen. Doctors may spend long hours on routine medical tests because there are no laboratory technicians.

Too Many Lawyers

The problem is not simply one of educating more people; it is one of educating them in the right direction. In much of Latin America, for example, there is an oversupply of lawyers. Everyone seems to want to be a lawyer. How do you persuade a young man to be an engineer instead?

In some underdeveloped countries, being able to read and write is considered enough. If you can read and write, you are educated. And—especially in former colonial nations—education is often regarded as a passport to a life of ease. If you can get an education, you can stop working. This does not mean that you merely stop physical labor, but that you can stop working altogether. Education will permit you to get along—if not get rich—without work. If the son of a peasant learns to read and write, it rarely occurs to him that he might have a better chance to succeed in agriculture with his new knowledge. He moves to the city to look for a position more suited to an educated man.

It was not long ago that a person in India who knew how to read and write considered himself superior to any job but the Indian civil service. Tens of thousands of Indians did no work at all rather than take an available job involving physical labor. The new found dignity of being an educated man was coupled with a feeling that the world owed an educated man a living simply because he was educated.

In the last generation or two, there has been a recognition in the developed world that the educated man owes society a great deal extra because he is educated. A wider understanding of this responsibility is needed in the underdeveloped world.

THE LAVISH UNIVERSITY

Veneration for education has other effects. In many underdeveloped countries, an ornate capitol building to symbolize newly won independence is the only thing more important than the creation of a magnificent university to show how cultured the country is. Slim educational resources are poured lavishly into the creation of a superb campus, with costly buildings and a big-name faculty. These the country cannot yet afford.

There is no question but that indigenous institutions of higher learning are desirable in the modernizing nations and every nation should have one as soon as possible. Yet resources for educational expansion are so slender that careful thought must be given to priorities. In most countries, this means that secondary education should have precedence over university education. To operate effectively, universities must have an underpinning of secondary schools in large numbers. While the secondary-school system is being developed, government scholarships can be provided for many advanced studies in universities outside the country. Such scholarships will cost considerably less than immediate expansion of local institutions of higher learning.

Furthermore, the symbolic university's usual purpose

is to grant degrees in philosophy, religion, liberal arts, or law. These are valuable disciplines, but they do not answer immediate needs for skills in engineering, the business and administrative arts, agriculture, and technical training. The university in a traditional society tends to be a special sanctum for philosophers and poets, anthropologists and archeologists, writers and dramatists, musicians and artists. The contributions these people make to humanity are vital and enormous, but many other disciplines are required for economic development in an underdeveloped nation.

NEW TECHNIQUES

Entirely new techniques may have to be employed if ignorance is to be conquered on the scale required, and in time. One such technique is teaching by radio. Used extensively for entertainment, culture, propaganda, and advertising in the industrially advanced world, radio's potential as a teaching tool—especially with a largely illiterate audience—has never been fully explored.

Some of the obstacles to a wide use of radio in the underdeveloped world are being tackled. Plans are already under way with UNESCO participation for the production of small portable radios powered by solar cells and costing little—one or two dollars at most. New developments show great promise of keeping the cost of transmitting stations down. Programs, plans, and methods of teaching by radio, however, are still not being adequately tested.

Another possibility is television and the motion picture. Working models of filmstrip projectors using the sun instead of electricity as a power source have been made.

Motion pictures and television offer tremendous opportunities in urban areas.

Programmed learning—the teaching-machine method—holds out promise of making each existing teacher in the underdeveloped world four or five or ten times as effective as he is now in traditional classrooms.

Meanwhile there can be greater interchange of teachers and students among nations. The Peace Corps—one example of an attempt to help in education and training—has been useful and will make an even greater contribution as it is expanded. Young men from Africa, Asia, and Latin America could be given on-the-job training and apprenticeship in established countries. Vocational training, teacher training, and adult education should be increased. There is no time to lose in getting on with all these important tasks, for much more education and training is indispensable if hunger and poverty, the handmaidens of ignorance, are to be conquered.

7

THE POPULATION EXPLOSION

POLITICAL scientists and economists are engaged in a great debate about how many people the earth can support. Considering known ways of producing food, arguments range from the promise that ten billion people can live on our planet to the gloomy statement that the three billion we now have are more than can ever be fed adequately.

That debate is likely to go on for some time. What we know for certain is that today about half the world does not have enough to eat, and the number of people is growing at a truly explosive rate.

Population growth tends to cancel economic growth. If the world's population increases 10 per cent during a period when its output of foods increases 10 per cent, the net benefit per person is zero. Many countries are having to run hard just to stand still.

A case in point is the Aswan high dam in Egypt—one of the most ambitious engineering undertakings in any underdeveloped nation. The predicted effects of its first phase will be to make available two million acres of new cropland. This is expected to raise agricultural production about 45 per cent.

It will take ten years to build the dam and install the irrigation canals. At the present rate the Egyptian population will then have increased enough to absorb nearly all the additions the dam will make to the country's food supply. Thus the net effect of the project, so far as food is concerned, will be that—while it will have prevented a disastrous decline in living standards—it will have added little to the lot of the average Egyptian. (The second phase of the project, to be completed ten years later, will triple the present production of electric power in Egypt. This, of course, will greatly stimulate the economy.)

REASONS FOR GROWTH

Why does population growth continue despite the fact that it keeps people poor? There are many reasons. One is that family planning is not feasible or acceptable in some countries. In others, where childless old age can mean starvation, children are a form of "social security"—indeed, the only form. Boys are a standard of value in a world which has no other material wealth. Girls are not only sources of domestic labor but they can often bring dowries which seem large in the family's eyes. Children are also symbols of prestige—however poorly they may be provided for.

But the number of children born is not the only and perhaps not the most important reason for over-all population growth. It can be argued that, except in certain industrially advanced nations, the birth rate today is about the same as it has always been. The declining death rate is more generally responsible for population growth.

Concerted attacks on diseases such as malaria and yaws have kept people alive longer. The result? Indonesia, to take one example, has almost doubled its population in the last twenty-seven years. India is growing annually by as many people as live in New York City. Between 1960 and 1970, the total population of the underdeveloped world will have increased by more than 300 million.

This "population explosion" is numerically frightening in itself. But it is intensified by a tragic shortage of housing. Roughly one billion people in Africa, Asia, and Latin America—about half the total population of these continents—are without real shelter, or live in unsafe, unhealthy, and overcrowded houses which are a hazard to their health and an affront to their dignity. In Nicaragua, 92.7 per cent of all rural dwellings have either one or two rooms. The average number of people per room in Guatemala—country and city—is three. The United Nations has estimated that no fewer than twenty million dwellings would have to be constructed in underdeveloped countries each year for the next thirty years in order to overcome existing shortages and provide for expected population growth.

CITIES PROVIDE NO REFUGE

Because conditions on the farm are so very primitive, people have been flocking to the cities to seek improvement. But this has proved to be an illusion. Some major cities have a squatter population as high as 20 to 30 per cent. These squatters have no clean water, no sewage disposal, and no steady jobs. Yet still they come; by 1970, the city population of Africa, Asia, and Latin America seems likely to increase by 200 million. Without careful planning and action immediately, the slums, shantytowns, sickness, disillusionment, misery, and social instability of the cities of tomorrow may break down orderly civic and national life.

It is government leadership which has, through health and sanitation measures, reduced the number of deaths; and it will also be for government leadership to take the first step of studying the country's population situation and trends in the context of its development plans.

In the low-income countries, where population increases are creating an insuperable problem of feeding, educating, and employing their people, the governments face an enormous task of research, education, and assistance. Extreme measures to slow down the population growth, such as sterilization and abortion, are unacceptable to many peoples. Any steps taken must be in line with the customs of the country.

Better means of fertility control can be developed. And here the advanced countries can help. By intensifying scientific investigations, they may find methods of effective control which are simple, safe, and cheap enough to be within the means of people wishing to use them. Possibilities include pills, inoculation, and immunization. The advanced nations can also aid countries that seek to control population growth, and request assistance in doing so, by helping to pay the costs of welfare services and necessary supplies.

It will obviously take a long time, even in the most favorable circumstances, for any serious impact to be made on the problem of excessively high rates of population increase. This makes all the more urgent the job of accelerating the pace of economic growth and social advancement in the underdeveloped world.

8

THE PLUNGE INTO THE
TWENTIETH CENTURY

Economic development is somewhat akin to building a motorcar. Not only must the parts be matched to each other—for example, a 200-h.p. engine should not be installed in a chassis designed for a 100-h.p. engine— but each part must also reach the assembly line at the right time. In development, too, balance and timing are essential.

India found this out the hard way; her second five-year plan over-concentrated on industrialization which proved disastrous for agricultural output. Her third five-year plan endeavors to correct the effects of this error.

Mainland China appears to be learning this lesson at great cost. Reports from there indicate that the Great Leap Forward has stubbed its toe on the simple fact that agricultural productivity and the creation of industrial capacity must go hand in hand. It is not feasible to concentrate on industry alone.

In the spring of 1962, Peiping is reported to have announced that five million Chinese were to be moved back to the farm from the factories and cities into which they had been recruited by the government in a headlong attempt to industrialize the economy. People cannot work in factories without food and fiber from the farms.

The slow pace of the industrial revolution in the United States may have concealed the fact that it was accompanied by a revolution in agriculture. The United States could not have industrialized as it did without better seeds, better land use, and better marketing, nor can any of the modernizing nations of today's world. They must achieve a balance between progress in agriculture and progress in industry if they are to succeed in economic development.

This balance—even in the industrially advanced nations—is precarious at best. The United States faces mammoth food surpluses and industrial unemployment at the same time. In parts of Europe too, food surpluses are within sight.

The underdeveloped world has the opposite problem: food scarcity. Agricultural production in much of this part of the world is at subsistence level or below.

THE TRAGEDY OF LOW PRODUCTIVITY

One of the most heart-rending facts apparent to a visitor is how pitifully little is produced by so much back-breaking labor. While in the United States a single farmer typically produces enough food for himself and for twenty-three non-food-producing persons, in many parts of Africa it takes from two to ten men, women, and children to produce barely enough for themselves and only one non-food-producing adult.

This imposes a vicious kind of self-perpetuating en-
slavement. The farmer cannot produce enough crops to
"get some extra." He cannot buy fertilizer to improve
his yield without the extra he cannot get. Until he can
produce more than just enough to get by, he cannot improve. It is like a snake swallowing its own tail; there is
no future in it.

Sari-Khatela is a village of some two thousand persons
on the road from New Delhi, India, to Agra, site of the
magnificent Taj Mahal. Its people live in *kacha,* or one-
room mud huts topped by thatched roofs. Buffalo and
oxen share the mud yards with barefoot children.

The villagers make their living growing sugar cane in
summer and wheat (and other grains) in winter. They
harvest their cane in October. Slack periods in field work
are spent grinding the cane into syrup, sugaring it off,
and selling the produce.

Oxen plod continuously in circles, turning fifteen-foot
handles attached to grinding machinery. A boy sits at each
machine feeding it the stalks. The syrup is led into bowls
and under each bowl is a blazing fire, built into the earth.
The sugar crystallizes into *gur,* a solid, grainy substance.

Twenty family groups keep busy in this fashion, until
it is time to harvest the wheat crop. Income from the sale
of *gur* amounts to roughly sixty-five cents a day per person,
which makes Sari-Khatela well off by Indian standards.
Its per capita income is three times as high as the national
average.

Given electricity, and even slightly more modern machinery, the village could emerge quickly from the Middle
Ages to the twentieth century. It could multiply many
fold its productivity, and hence its standard of living.

Clearly, this problem of productivity is at the heart of

economic development. Better seed, more land, better methods, some basic tools, better markets can all lead to higher agricultural output. As more food is produced, some of it can be used for others as well as for the family unit. A portion may be useful for export—to produce needed foreign exchange.

Increased agricultural productivity also makes possible an improvement in conditions of rural life, so that young people will want to "stay on the farm" rather than migrate to crowded cities where opportunities for useful employment may not yet exist.

This necessity for a transformation in farm productivity is sometimes overlooked by countries seeking to pull themselves up by their bootstraps. There is a tendency to reach out for something dramatic, like a steel mill, in the hope of suddenly achieving a golden future.

PLANNING FOR INDUSTRY

It is also necessary, of course, for a developing nation to give attention to industry. No country wishes to be solely a nation of farmers, living a hand-to-mouth existence, dependent upon caprices of soil and weather. Industrialization opens a spiraling opportunity to acquire capital and reinvest it in further capital-producing activities.

So great has been the eagerness for industrialization, however—so glittering has been the pot of gold at the end of the rainbow—that unproductive factories have been built. What most developing countries really need—and what many of them have come to see they need—is a large number of small-scale industries, rural as well as urban, suited to the talents and resources of the people.

Many handicrafts help to introduce industrial organization and techniques into predominantly agricultural societies; they represent a first step toward industrialization. Not only do they add to the income of the people, they help to collect and use whatever capital and skills exist in rural areas.

Governments can do much to encourage rural industries and village handicrafts. They can give a low priority to the construction of factories that might compete unduly with them. They can encourage village cooperatives and provide credit facilities. They can make electric power available. Most of Denmark's present industries grew out of cottage handicrafts aided by new mechanical power.

First steps to heavy industry should be taken with care. Automatic machines or techniques may be judged best in some instances, bypassing the need to learn a skill which would be needed only for a short time. But use of obsolete equipment may serve to teach skills without which adoption of modern machinery would be a waste.

KALEIDOSCOPIC CHANGE

There is too the question of national stability. In many parts of the underdeveloped world, poverty has been the way of life since time immemorial. With this poverty—perhaps as part of it—has come a traditional stability. Things could not get worse; they did not get better.

Now that stability is disappearing. The one constant of a modernizing nation is change. Nothing will be the same tomorrow as it is today. The industrially advanced nations have gone through this development in slow stages, with each generation able to inherit a modified attitude and add to it. In the modernizing nations of today, this experience will be condensed into one or two generations, with resulting friction and upheaval. Like men coming suddenly out of a cave into bright sunlight, they will be dazzled by their new environment.

Some countries, notably India, are attempting to ease the transition by sending trained men and women into each village and town, like "county agents" in the United States generations ago, to teach the people how to do things more effectively. They help them set up primary schools and adult-literacy courses. They teach hygiene. They demonstrate new seeds and tools, actually working the ground themselves to prove what can be done. They show how fertilizers and pesticides should be used. They introduce small hand industries. Sometimes they set up village marketing cooperatives, build roads, dig wells, erect schools.

Since October 1952, when the Indian government first started sending out such grass-roots workers, 400,000 villages have been affected (out of a total of 558,000 in the country). No fewer than 300 million Indian farmers (out of 330 million) have been helped by 80,000 community workers. And the idea is spreading in other parts of Asia.

INDUSTRIAL ESTATES

A novel and interesting method of stimulating small- and medium-scale industries, being tried in India and elsewhere in Asia, is to establish "industrial estates," areas which contain power, water, common workshops, advisory services—all the facilities the budding entrepreneur needs to try out his wings in manufacturing. He rents a factory within the estate. If he succeeds, he may eventually grow to need his own grounds; if he fails, he will not have lost as much as he would if he had built his own plant.

The concept of an industrial estate has been carried further by some countries, including India, to an industrial "community." Here, there are social services and housing as well. Both "estates" and "communities" can force the location of industry into orderly patterns, instead of the sprawling, illogical arrangement typical of so many advanced countries. They can often provide greater efficiency and economy.

Something of the kind, indeed, was pioneered in the American West when railroad construction outfits set up spurs and industrial sites along the railroad tracks and leased them to industry. At the turn of the century, water from the Niagara River was led by canals to newly established industrial sites on the American side and fed over individual water wheels, each entrepreneur having his own water wheel. This was the first way in which Niagara power was put to use.

The United Nations has spread traditional and modern approaches to industrialization. A number of promising industries in the underdeveloped areas today owe their existence at least in part to the United Nations.

A penicillin plant near Bombay provides one example. In the beginning, the project was plagued by a multitude of troubles. The workers did not know what to do or how to do it. Some routines normally expected of a factory worker in an industrially advanced nation were incomprehensible to the men engaged to operate the penicillin plant.

One by one the problems were licked. When it became evident that the plant was going to be successful, a number of other plants sprang up around it. One supplied boxes. Another produced packaging for the penicillin. Still others produced supplies needed for the manufacturing process. The supporting operations were financed and managed by private individuals who saw a market and had the imagination and capacity to take advantage of it. Success had generated success.

TRANSPORT AND ELECTRIC POWER

Industrial plans can go only as far as a country's transport and electric power will take them. Products have to be brought to markets. Tourism is the only business which benefits from scenic grandeur; and even then, some system of getting tourists in and accommodating them during their stay is necessary.

Even in countries like Mexico and Turkey which are well along in the development process, uneven transport planning has hurt industry's chances. In both countries industrial centers have been forced to concentrate around the seaports, which provide the only ready outlets. Meanwhile, other parts of those countries are deprived of the higher standard of living that industry can bring.

Lack of adequate transport divides whole continents into isolated segments. Save for the luxury of air travel, most African countries have no easy link to each other, no tangible basis for creating regional markets. Parts of Latin America are no closer to each other today than they were a century ago. The same is true of Asia.

Plans exist now for an Asian highway, as well as for rail and water links. Africa is beginning to plan in the same direction. Because these are bold and ambitious projects, we must not treat them as utopian goals to be achieved in some vague tomorrow. Unless there are great advances in transport in the immediate future, development of agriculture as well as industry will suffer.

Electric power is equally crucial. With increased mechanization, manufacturing depends more and more on local power facilities. Large concerns may generate this power for themselves, but smaller units, which usually pioneer in the industrialization process, require purchasable power.

In most areas the electricity-generating capacity of the less-developed countries is wholly insufficient for their needs. The United States and other industrially advanced countries produce 93.2 per cent of the world's electric power. Australia and New Zealand alone produce more than the whole of Asia, except for Japan, even though their combined populations are only some thirteen million as against 1,445,894,000.

In their attempts to overcome this disparity, the underdeveloped countries face severe problems. Power facilities cannot be gradually increased, at small cost, to meet growing demand. They must be laid down in complex and costly units. There is no such thing as half a dam.

If governments want power, therefore, they must be prepared for heavy investment. On the other hand, do they want to divert to this use capital which, at an early stage, could perhaps be used still more beneficially elsewhere in the economy? Consider this dilemma in terms of the commitments that some low-income countries are making for atomic energy installations. Atomic power may well be the long-range answer to their problems. But at present it is much more expensive in most places than traditional power. By starting now, a government may complete its atomic power plant just when the use of atomic energy becomes feasible and economical; but there is a

big gamble involved. And what about the years in between?

There is no blanket answer applicable to all cases.
Some investment capital must be available for energy production and distribution. But power must take its place
alongside transport, industry, commerce, and agriculture
in a balanced program for integrated development.

9

THE EMPTY SAVINGS BANK

THE IDEA of saving today to build a better tomorrow is virtually unknown in countries where today's supply is desperately meager. It is difficult for a man whose belt is already pulled in beyond the last notch to tighten it any further. Yet as every farmer knows, out of even a small harvest some grain must be saved for a new and larger planting. There must be something in the bank if tomorrow is ever to be brighter.

Underdeveloped countries suffer from a paralyzing lack of capital. This lack is one of the basic obstacles to growth. It is capital which is the fulcrum of production—capital in the shape of plows, tools, engines, cranes, factories, warehouses, dams. Without capital, a man is limited to what he can produce with his ingenuity and the strength of his bare hands, plus the most primitive equipment— stick plows, oxcarts, hand-dug irrigation ditches, hand-turned spinning wheels.

It is lack of capital which cripples the postage-stamp farmer. Peasants working their tiny strips of land cannot afford steel plows to replace their wooden ones. Chemical

fertilizer is impossibly expensive for hand-to-mouth budgets, and even animal fertilizer is scarce. Nor is capital
available in the form of draft animals.

One revealing index of the scarcity of capital is the
availability of useful power in the underdeveloped lands.
In India in 1953, man and beast produced 65 per cent of
all the nation's energy, and of the remaining 35 per cent—
i.e., of the inanimately-produced energy—about three-
quarters was secured from the burning of animal dung.
In the United States, in the same year, human and animal
power together accounted for only 1 per cent of the nation's energy, and the use of primitive animal fuels was
practically zero. The total amount of electric power generated by India in 1953 for over four hundred million
people would not have sufficed to light up New York City;
and despite a doubling of production since that time
India's electricity output on a per capita basis is still less
than 2 per cent of that of the United States.

THE CORE OF THE PROBLEM

This deep-rooted problem of capital shortage is at the
heart of the whole problem of overcoming poverty. Certain things, of course, can be done without money. In
many of the low-income countries, highways are constructed, wells dug, and houses built by cooperative community action. But development generally involves trans-
actions in which money is used—either local currency or
foreign exchange.

The local currency must come from taxes imposed by
governments, from borrowing by governments, and from
private earnings. All this is easier said than done in a
country where up to 60 per cent of the people are going

hungry. How can savings for investment be acquired under such circumstances? This is one of the most pervasive dilemmas of the underdeveloped world.

No solution is presently in sight. During the 1950s, in nearly two-thirds of the underdeveloped countries, domestic savings did not rise at all in relation to gross national product. Indeed, in half of them it declined. Where it did rise, the increase was usually modest. Despite the enormous difficulties, such governments will have to take urgent measures to increase local savings and channel them into productive projects. There is also a need for tax reform. Somehow, the domestic bank must be filled.

THE NEED FOR FOREIGN EXCHANGE

Even assuming maximum self-help, however, low-income countries still need foreign exchange. Many essentials simply cannot be purchased with local currency. There must be some way to buy the goods and services that can come only from abroad.

The first and best source of foreign exchange is a country's own export trade. To the extent that it sells abroad, it can buy abroad. It is dependent, however, on the willingness and ability of richer countries to buy its goods.

A recession or depression in an industrialized nation often has more impact on the underdeveloped countries than on the industrialized nation itself. For example, the 1957–1958 economic recession that began in the United States and spread to Western Europe drove down raw material prices and reduced the export earnings of the underdeveloped countries by 7 to 8 per cent from mid-1957 to mid-1958. During the same period the prices of manufactured goods, even in an industrial recession, continued to rise with the result that the underdeveloped countries were caught in a squeeze and lost about $2 billion in import capacity. This was almost as much as all the foreign aid they received in the period, and was approximately equivalent to six years' lending by the World Bank to the underdeveloped countries at 1956–1957 rates.

To meet the deficit in their earnings the countries had to run their foreign exchange reserves down to dangerous levels, turn to overseas borrowing, and, in many cases, reduce imports severely. In effect, the underdeveloped countries were making a subsidy or contribution to the industrialized countries at a time when those advanced countries were trying to aid the development of the low-income countries through grants and loans. Such a situation obviously makes no sense.

One of the reasons why many Latin Americans grew so hostile to the United States in 1958 and 1959 was that their countries' exports to the United States were falling off in volume and value while the prices of the things they bought from the United States were rising. This kind of pinch hits the pocketbooks of millions of people.

Problems arising from fickle markets in the industrialized countries persisted into mid-1961 when the late Dag Hammarskjold, then UN secretary-general, pointed to the paradox that the industrial nations' "progressive expansion of aid has not been matched by equal progress in the reduction in obstacles to the growth of trade."

THE UN'S FINDINGS

For more than a decade the United Nations has been concerned with these problems. It has made many studies of trade policies and the commodity-price problem. These studies concluded: (1) that international price-stabilization schemes for primary commodities are extremely hard to arrange and difficult to administer; (2) that combined national and international price-stabilization programs, however, can and do cushion price fluctuations in a few commodities (e.g., sugar, wheat, and tin) and should be tried in others; (3) that the less-developed countries should try not to depend on just one or two exports, but should diversify their economies; (4) but that even under the best conditions, recession or depression in the industrially advanced countries can undo all the good of price stabilization schemes and diversification.

It is clearly folly for rich countries to pour in aid and investment at the top of the barrel while pursuing policies that allow the low-income countries' own substance to drain out at the bottom.

For instance—

1. Coffee, tea, cocoa, tropical fruits, and other "luxury" commodities produced in vast quantities in low-income countries are taxed so heavily in many industrialized countries that sales are sharply reduced.

2. Many industrialized nations limit imports of farm products so as to maintain artificially high domestic prices or otherwise protect their own agriculture.

3. Many industrialized countries impose tariffs, excise taxes, or quantitative limitations on imports of some industrial raw materials which are the mainstays of the economies of underveloped countries (e.g., United States restrictions on imports of lead and zinc).

4. Many industrialized countries, although admitting raw materials free, impose restrictive duties upon imports

of those same commodities when they are in even slightly
processed form.

5. Low-income countries frequently are forbidden to
sell manufactured goods to industrialized countries, or
find the door almost completely closed, on the ground
that the goods are produced with cheap labor.

Trade restrictions of this kind not only penalize con-
sumers in the industrialized countries but also curtail the
ability of low-income countries to improve their lot. Rich
countries frequently advise poor ones to help themselves;
but these appeals have a hollow ring when the person being exhorted is not allowed to help himself. In these circumstances, foreign aid to low-income countries may only
serve to compensate, wholly or partially, for the opportunities for self-improvement which have been denied
him. To restrict trade while extending aid is thus like
beating a man with one hand while dressing his wounds
with the other.

POSSIBLE REMEDIES

The United Nations is considering two possible reme-
dies for the price squeeze in which underdeveloped countries periodically get caught. One is the creation of an insurance fund that would come to the rescue of a country
whose only source of livelihood had suddenly been
knocked from under it.

The other is price control for certain selected commodities. Much the same kind of program—crop insurance
and price stabilization—has been tried in some countries,
notably the United States, to protect farmers from serious
loss or bankruptcy.

Even if all these problems are solved, however—even if

trade channels are opened wide and prices are stabilized
—low-income countries will still be unable for some time
to earn all the foreign exchange they need by selling their
products abroad. There must be other sources of capital—
notably loans and investments from abroad. How they can
get this capital—how they can finish the job of financing
their development—will be discussed in the following
chapters.

10

PROBING THE UNKNOWN

If A MAN HAS, say, $1,000 to invest, he is likely to put it to work where the chances of making a profit are best. Unless he thinks he can get a fabulous return, he is not likely to gamble on something wholly unproven.

Governments and institutions operate on the same principle. They are not inclined to speculate. There are, they know, rich opportunities to make money investing in many underdeveloped countries. These countries have great untapped resources waiting to be developed. But the "sure things" are all but gone, and until new ones are found, capital will be hesitant to venture forth.

The man who can uncover a proven opportunity for sound investment is doing a favor to both the investor and to the country which has the untapped wealth. The country gets desperately needed capital; the man or the institution with money learns how to use it profitably.

Searching for investment opportunity is known as "pre-investment" work. Its value has been proven time and time again. The UN Special Fund went into Argentina in 1959 and 1960 to find out where electric power was most needed, and where it could be produced. The survey cost the United Nations $300,000. Spending only that much, British and American engineers and economists found ways in which no less than $735 million could be profitably invested over a ten-year period to provide urgently needed electricity for Argentine industry and homes. The ratio between opportunity for investment and "seed money" was well over 2,000 to 1. As this book is being written, $300 million in investment capital has actually been put on the line. Indeed, it leapt at the opportunity.

Not all pre-investment work is so spectacularly successful. But I have found that a ratio of 100 to 1 between investment opportunity and seed money is not unusual; indeed, it is the average.

A Modern Treasure Hunt

Pre-investment in the underdeveloped countries means that a whole new world of potential wealth is being opened up. Most such countries have no idea of the extent or nature of their resources. They do not have accurate surveys of their land. They may not even know the size of their population. Groping in the dark, they are tempted to launch development projects based more on guesswork, hope, and public relations value than on sound blueprints for success.

Hundreds of millions of precious development dollars— and *rupees* and *cruzeiros* and *francs*—can go down the drain for lack of adequate investigation and project preparation. A lot of money has, in fact, been lost this way.

Failure of development schemes, however, is nothing compared to the losses the underdeveloped countries are suffering through not using their resources to the full.

There are dozens of rivers flowing through the low-income countries whose waters have never been used for irrigation or the generation of power. There are hundreds of millions of acres of land which could be made productive by the application of fertilizer. And there are other hundreds of millions of acres in semi-arid countries which could be made productive if ways were found to conserve river water that now flows into the sea unused, or to take the salt out of the sea water inexpensively.

Indonesia, for example, is blessed with a fertile volcanic soil and has much underground wealth that she has never exploited. South America has vast arable lands not now being used and great mineral potential. Africa boasts huge reserves of subsoil treasure. Libya, a barren desert, would have been written off as a nation almost bereft of any of the gifts of nature. Today she is known to have substantial oil deposits. Underdeveloped countries, generally speaking, are not poor in resources. They are poor in knowledge of their resources.

THE MAGIC OF SCIENCE

Science and technology have come to our aid in spectacular fashion in this field of exploring the unknown. Every day, modern aerial photography—an extraordinary science—reveals resources hitherto concealed by precipitous mountain ranges, dense forests, desert sand, and inaccessible mudflats. The old-time intrepid prospector with his mule and pick has been relegated to the Hollywood film library and to history.

Fifty years ago it would have taken 220 years to conduct a thorough geographical survey of the United States. It is possible today, using low-flying planes and modern reconnaissance equipment, to do it in less than ten years. Other smaller countries can be surveyed in a matter of months.

Aerial cameras, supplemented by magnetometers, scintillation counters, and electromagnetic units, can identify types of soil and disclose the probable presence of twelve to fifteen different minerals underneath it. They can provide invaluable information on forests, geological formations, and land use. French planes using these techniques discovered a likelihood of oil in a part of the Sahara after explorers on camels had rejected the area as hopeless. Later, when the area was drilled, it proved to have some of the richest oil deposits in the world.

In some areas, airplanes afford the only possible, or at least the only feasible, method of exploration. It would cost far too much to cut through thick jungle, mile after mile, merely in the hope of finding mineral wealth. Aerial reconnaissance is expensive too—the planes, the instruments, the highly qualified personnel—but alternative methods would be a lot more costly. And the results are remarkable.

The UN Special Fund is making eight airborne geophysical studies to investigate mineral resources in hitherto virtually inaccessible and unproductive parts of Chile, Surinam, Bolivia, Mexico, Togo, Uganda, Somalia, and North Borneo. It is also making sixteen other "open-sky" surveys to study soil values, forests, and water resources. It is even exploring parts of Peru and Ecuador to find out whether they are suitable for human habitation.

THE PEACEFUL ATOM

Atomic energy is another exciting new tool for discovery. Harmless radioactive isotopes are giving a previously unthought of speed and accuracy to ground-water investigations. The old-fashioned method of seeking water with a willow wand is practical no more. It has been overtaken by the peaceful atom.

Radio isotopes also can be used nowadays to measure the speed of a swiftly flowing river or the infinitesimal movement in the veins of a leaf. Both processes are being used in United Nations' projects.

Previously, estimates of river flow were obtained by setting up speed gauges on the river banks, and by introducing color dyes into the water upstream and later measuring the color density at a downstream check point. This process often led to misleading conclusions about the influences of the river bed, the direction and speed of the flow, the connection between water sources in the area, and the position and size of natural underground reservoirs.

Nuclear research methods are being used in a UN agricultural project in Yugoslavia. By introducing infinitesimal quantities of harmless radioactive material into fertilizer, it will be possible to ascertain how quickly the fertilizer enters the plant and to judge how much fertilizer is required for different types of soil and for different types of cultivation.

Nor is even this all. Mechanical computers can actually build models of power dams, showing where the dam should be built, how high it should be, of what materials it should be made, and a hundred other things.

I do not mean to suggest that these new tools are by themselves miracle workers. The miracle lies in the hands and the minds that control them. After aerial surveys, groundwork has still to be done—but we know where to do it. After atomic tracers have shown what is happening in the river beds, we still have to plan and carry out the control programs. Before the computer can build the mathematical model, it has still to be fed data from measurements obtained slowly and painfully by men trudging through swamps and streams.

Even with all the advantages science can muster, the opening up of underdeveloped areas is still a matter of stout endeavor, of back-breaking toil, of human endurance, and of skill. But scientific techniques can speed up economic development in modernizing countries and transform the slow evolution of centuries into a matter of decades. It can make man's efforts incomparably more effective.

NIGERIA LOOKS AHEAD

An example of a rich but little used resource is the Niger River in western Africa. A study of ways to use a section of that river within Nigeria was completed by the United Nations in 1960. British and Dutch firms employed to make the survey discovered that the site selected earlier as best for a dam was unsuitable. An excellent new site was found at Kainji, and the report recommended that work begin immediately there so Nigeria can have the electricity it needs as soon as 1966.

If the UN blueprint is followed, the scheme will permit hydroelectric power production at an installed capacity of 860 megawatts, 22 per cent more than the Grand Coulee and substantially more than any dam in Western Europe. This is enough to satisfy the electricity requirements of Nigeria, so far as anyone can foresee them, for nearly twenty years.

Building the dam would benefit the people in other ways as well. It would provide an alternative crossing of

the Niger, thereby reducing traffic delays at the inadequate single-track railway bridge at Jabba. That bridge
is now used not only by trains but by automobiles, pedestrians, and cattle. The huge lake formed by the reservoir
would provide a much needed increase of protein from
fish production. Navigation on the river would be improved—upstream into neighboring Niger, and downstream to the sea.

Prospects for farming would be transformed through
the control of floods. On large areas of the flood plain,
intensive agriculture would become possible, particularly
with a pump irrigation system that would use Niger
waters stored up during the wet season, permitting cultivation of crops during the dry season. Net returns on the
crops would be increased by cheap transportation on the
river.

The dam, with generating and distribution equipment,
would cost about $22 million, part of which would come
from domestic sources. All initial capital from outside
sources could be repaid over a period of twenty years from
earnings on the sale of the electricity alone. The profit
would also be large enough to pay for an extension of the
generating capacity in later years. Present electricity rates
in Nigeria could be reduced substantially.

Instances of the kind could fill this book. One of Ethio-
pia's principal rivers is the Awash. Its waters have been
little used. Yet preliminary UN studies indicate that, with
control and efficient use of the river, the Awash valley can
become one of the most fertile in all of Africa. Prospects
are so bright that a British syndicate has signed an agree-
ment with the Ethiopian government to supply $35 mil-
lion for a development project in a part of the valley,
provided the intensive soil and water-use survey now un-

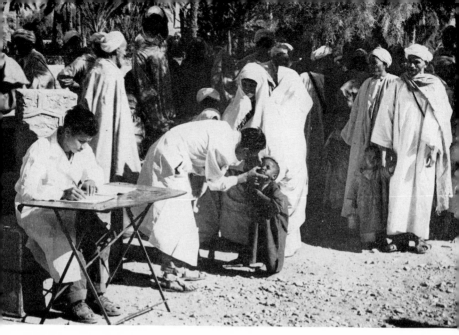

The mass campaign against conjunctivitis and trachoma is carried into the small villages of Morocco to protect over 100,000 tribesmen from the blinding disease.

Still swathed in traditional dress, these women are nevertheless emerging from the shadows to take their diplomas at the Health Center in the capital of Yemen.

WHO

The world over, UN experts are helping to see that food supplies are better used and the earth's resources more efficiently developed. Here is a demonstration of new farming equipment in Libya.

Two members of the International Atomic Energy Agency's scientific staff introducing tritium-labeled water into an underground system in Greece. This part of an investigation into groundwater resources of the Peloponnese is carried on within the framework of a Special Fund–FAO project.

Boys in Kenya learn a trade. Africa, like other rapidly developing countries, is facing the problems that come with urbanization, such as juvenile delinquency and vagrancy. Youth Centers to provide guidance and vocational training are supported by government, local agencies and business firms, and the United Nations Children's Fund.

"Open your book." A priest, Father Joaquin Salcedo, starting with a homemade radio transmitter and three receivers, has had remarkable success in bringing education to rural communities of Colombia. An FM antenna is supported by the cross and loudspeakers are girded to the dome of this belfry.

UNESCO—Paul Almasy
United Nations

der way with United Nations assistance measures up to the preliminary findings.

It's Really Nothing New

In the industrially advanced world, planning for economic development—i.e., pre-investment planning—has been commonplace for a long time. We have learned, often at great cost to the taxpayer, that highway systems, for example, must be planned with the greatest care. Planning involves a study of terrain, calculation of traffic flow, consideration of the durability of materials, availability of labor, weather records, and many other factors. Such preliminary planning costs money, but in the long run it saves many times as much money as it costs.

Theodore Schultz reported in the *Humanist*, a few years ago, a study of what hybrid-corn research had cost society and what return it had given.*

The history of hybrid-corn development in this country [the United States] goes back to 1910. . . .
A colleague of mine [Professor Zvi Griliches] has just published the results of some very ingenious research; he has found that if we count all of the private and public costs of hybrid-corn—everything that has gone into its development; and the records on this are quite complete—a total of $130,-000,000 has been invested since 1910. . . .
Then if we measure all of the product that can be identified and attributed to this particular new piece of useful knowledge, we find that its contribution to the consumer surplus, which is what made the analysis so difficult and required so much ingenuity, turns out to be no less than $910,000,000. That is, the return on the $130,000,000 invested is running at 700% per year.

* Schultz, "Human Wealth and Economic Growth," *The Humanist*, Vol. XIX, No. 2 (March–April 1959), pp. 71–81.

The case of hybrid-corn illustrates another fact: that new discoveries often have an impact far beyond the land of their birth. United Nations technicians, seeking to assist Yugoslavia in raising its farm output, turned to the United States for hybrid-corn seed to maximize production. From 1951 through 1955, the Yugoslav corn harvest had averaged 3,350,000 tons. The 1957 production, with the new seed, exceeded 5,500,000 tons, and in 1959, production broke through to a new peak of 6,670,000 tons. As the yields increased, acreages planted in corn could be transferred to other crops, including forage which would enrich the soil and provide foodstuffs required for livestock. There were crop setbacks in 1960, but they were traceable to entirely different causes.

PERSPECTIVE

Pre-investment, then, is a proven boon. How much should be spent on it?

In 1962, about $600 million in all was being put to this use from outside sources. Of this amount, the United Nations and its specialized agencies were handling about $150 million. The rest was largely direct government-to-government aid, although private foundations and other groups made notable contributions.

The over-all total should nearly double by 1970. I believe that $1 billion is the very minimum that we should be devoting to pre-investment work by the end of this decade. The United Nations, with its obvious advantages, could usefully handle at least $400 million of this amount. Thus, the United Nations' share should be more than doubled, and the more quickly this is done, the better.

Virtually all countries—at least ninety of the one hundred discussed here—can extract enough from their soil, their water, and the talents of their people to lick poverty, hunger, ignorance, and disease. No country is too poor to better itself substantially. Nature has, of course, distributed its bounties unevenly; development will be more difficult in some places than others. Some countries should concentrate on animal husbandry, others on rice culture. Some countries should make coal a source of energy, some oil. What they all have in common is a need to map out the path, to know what they have and where they are going.

11

LIBYA: A MICROCOSM

LIBYA, FACING Italy and Greece from the southern shore of the Mediterranean Sea, is roughly twice the size of Texas. No less than 97 per cent of its 680,000 square miles is desert sand. Mile after dreary mile of dunes and sandstone stretch southward from the sea to the blistering Sahara. Summer temperatures of 135 degrees have been recorded in Tripoli when the Ghibli, or south wind, whips in from the desert.

Libya was probably the poorest self-governing country in the world when it gained its independence in December 1951. The average income per person was roughly $35 a year. Eighty-five per cent of the people could neither read nor write. Nomads roamed the countryside or lived in miserable huts and tents. Such little wealth as there was had been seriously damaged or destroyed when World War II swept across North Africa. Much of the grazing area was still spotted with live land mines, left behind by the forces of Field Marshal Rommel, the "Desert Fox," and by the Allied armies.

Libya had not been truly independent since the fall of

Carthage in 146 B.C. Its most recent overlord had been Fascist Italy. Under the terms of the World War II peace treaty between the Allied powers and Italy, the United States, Britain, France, and the Soviet Union were given the task of deciding Libya's future. If they could not agree within one year, the decision was to be left to the United Nations General Assembly. The four powers did in fact reach a deadlock, and the matter was referred to the UN. The UN decided to set up Libya as an independent country, the deadline for independence being January 1, 1952. Actually, independence was proclaimed December 24, 1951.

Having assumed a kind of parental responsibility, the UN General Assembly set out to care for its offspring. Even before independence, a United Nations Advisory Council under Commissioner Adrian Pelt of the Netherlands, with Thomas F. Power, Jr., an American, as his deputy, went to the country. The Assembly had conceived of Libya's independence mainly as a political undertaking, but Pelt immediately saw much wider needs. He sent an SOS back to Secretary-General Trygve Lie for a team of experts to plan the country's economic and social development.

A KINGDOM IS CREATED

A committee of Libyans with the commissioner's help drew up a proposed constitution. After intermediate preparatory steps, a National Assembly was convened to consider it. From all corners of the country, the assemblymen came—on foot from the coastal provinces, by mule and camel from the desert Fezzan. Tribal differences were submerged, a federal monarchy was set up, and the Emir of

Cyrenaica was unanimously proclaimed King Idris I of a united Libya.

Meanwhile the team of UN experts began arriving. Its members set out to analyze the country's desperately impoverished economy to see what could be done to put it on a sound basis. After careful research and study, the members came up with a series of reports which they molded into a detailed plan. Then, with the government's approval, Libya and the UN set out to put these and related ideas into action.

There were practically no trained people to run the government or to operate factories and workshops. There were not even any typists, stenographers, or clerical workers for many government offices. So one of the first actions the United Nations took was to call in UNESCO, the UN's educational arm, and later, the International Labor Organization, skilled in training workmen, to set up a Technical and Clerical Training Center. Boys were invited to come and were offered two, three, or four years of schooling, with free board, room, and tuition, in return for a pledge that after graduation they would work for the government for at least two years. The UN and the provisional government shared the cost.

NEW CLOTHES FOR SOME

The boys arrived, most of them barefoot, usually with one ragged cotton garment to their name. The UN gathered some new (or newer) clothing to give them, but there was not enough for everyone. How to decide whom to help? It was decided that if a man could put his fist through the largest hole in the boy's clothing, the boy was eligible for new clothes. If only a few fingers would go through, the clothes would have to do.

Of the first class, 93 per cent were found to have the eye disease, trachoma, which can lead to blindness. Since half of the boys were to be clerks and office workers, this was a serious matter. The UN got in contact with an American foreign-aid team which was battling this disease, and the boys were given daily treatment.

The other half of the students at the school—the total began with about one hundred and soon had to expand; three to four times as many boys applied as could be admitted—were trained to be artisans. Many had never seen a machine of any kind in their lives, or even any tool except the simplest hand tool. The ILO taught them how to be welders, blacksmiths, metal-turners, fitters and joiners, and even automobile mechanics and electricians. They proved to have remarkable aptitudes for the work.

One such school in a country of one million people where six out of every seven people could neither read nor write could be only a drop in the bucket. So the government set out to build a public-education system, with massive help from the United Nations and a number of bilateral programs. Of eight hundred teachers in Tripolitania province, it was found, two hundred had themselves only been through the first or second grades. Another four hundred had had two to four years of schooling, and no training at all in how to teach. UNESCO assigned specialists to improve two teacher-training colleges, one in Tripoli and the other in Bengazi. At first it was difficult to get any girls to come and study; traditionally, women and girls were heavily veiled, and confined strictly to the home. Only nineteen girls were found for the first UN class in

Tripoli, taught by a Palestinian woman. But the next year, as word got around, three hundred came to enroll and more than one hundred had to be turned away.

SCHOOLS MODERNIZED

The public-school system was primitive. A typical school had some sixty-five or seventy first-grade pupils, all boys. They had perhaps ten books and five or ten pencils to share among them. There were no desks; the pupils would sit on benches, or on the floor. They would be told to fold their arms, keep quiet, and repeat in turn the lessons dictated by the teacher.

Now, in large part as a result of work done by a UNESCO expert, Adeline Babbitt of Hawaii and New York, model demonstration schools have been set up. Teaching methods are being modernized, school furniture has been built in the right size for the little children, and books, pencils, crayons, and paper have been supplied—some of it with American aid money, some by the government, some by the United Nations. One UN official, describing a visit to these schools, said the children "are bright-eyed and just as eager and interested and capable of absorbing their lessons as those in some of the best schools anywhere." The number of pupils is multiplying fast—and there are thousands of girls among them.

At the time of independence 45,000 children went to school; on the tenth anniversary of independence the Federal Minister of Education announced that the number had gone up to 170,000.

Meanwhile something had to be done to help more Libyans earn a decent living. More than 87 per cent of the people work on the land, so this was a job for which the United Nations Food and Agriculture Organization was specially qualified. The FAO began by bringing in fifteen experts to look over what was being done and see how it could be done better.

Libya had been one of the granaries of the Roman Empire. But over the centuries the wells filled with sand, and neglect, deforestation, and the relentless onrush of the desert had largely denuded the land. Goats, camels, and sheep had been allowed to eat grass which had held down the thin soil, and the wind had blown it away. Here and there, remains of Roman farmhouses could be seen in areas which once must have been covered with olive trees and arable land, but by the mid-twentieth century had become barren desert.

BATTLING THE DESERT

One of the first things the FAO set out to do was to drive back the desert. At the suggestion of an FAO forestry expert from France, the provincial government of Tripolitania planted more than 1.5 million trees. Recently the number was raised to three million. It began fixing sand dunes, also at his suggestion, by planting a special type of grass which would grow in the sand. Shelter-belts were mapped and set up around the city of Tripoli; the desert was literally held back, and farm areas began to improve in value. A twenty-five- to thirty-year battle may be necessary to bring the desert fully under control, but Libya has begun.

Next the FAO turned to sources of farm income. The backbone of the country's economy had been the export of some two thousand tons of wool a year. It was not a very good quality wool, since the sheep had little to eat in the summer. Also, it was not sorted and cleaned properly, and thus brought low prices on the foreign market.

The FAO brought in an Australian sheep-breeding expert to demonstrate how to feed the flocks, breed them for greater endurance, and treat them for insect pests and parasites. The government provided funds to supply three hundred sheep for each of two demonstration stations on government-owned property. There Libyan farmers came and saw how to care for their flocks. They watched the sheep being put through chemical baths to kill the insects. At first the farmers were skeptical, but then they began bringing in their own flocks for treatment, until the animals were flowing through by the thousands—and the quality of the flocks was improving materially. The FAO also imported 150 sheep from Turkey to see how that particular type would adapt to conditions in Libya. New, scientific breeding policies were instituted. The production of a better quality wool enabled ILO to start in the Fezzan a school where boys are being trained in the art of carpet weaving. Today Fezzan carpets fetch good prices in Tripoli and are becoming an export article.

AN INDUSTRY REVIVED

Another important small industry in Libya is the tanning of goat, sheep, and camel skins and hides. The traditional method of removing the hide from an animal and preparing it for tanning produced skins that were weak, scarred, and filled with holes. A UN expert showed farmers how to do it in such a way as to produce a good, firm skin; and he introduced a grading system which helped to standardize exports.

The new product was tried out in British, American, and Italian markets and found to sell much more readily —and bring better prices. Orders from glove-makers and other leather-users began coming in. All through the industry—among the butchers, the flayers, the curers, and the skin merchants—there was lively new activity. Concrete floors were put in to provide for better drainage; new tools were purchased, and new people trained. The industry got a new lease on life.

Libya is a big potential producer of oranges, grapefruit, lemons, and many other kinds of fruit. The coastal belt along the Mediterranean has a soil and climate that are particularly suitable. Millions of trees had been planted by the Italians, but the plantations had been partially abandoned after World War II and large numbers of trees wiped out. Many had been cut for firewood. Libya was actually having to import fresh fruit.

The FAO brought in a horticultural expert from Jordan, where the climate and terrain are not dissimilar. He first proposed that experimental stations, nurseries, and run-down plantations be rehabilitated and used for demonstration purposes. Then one such station was planted with almonds, olives, and citrus fruit and others with vines, olives, figs, and apples. Dry-farming methods were demonstrated. The United States aid mission set up a number of other such demonstration farms.

It had been impossible, up to this time, to market Libyan citrus fruit in Europe, because it was not graded to standard sizes, and because it was infested with the Mediterranean fruit fly and with a black fungus growth. No European country would let in such fruit, especially when its own orchards might become infested as a result. A UN plant-protection expert from Switzerland showed

farmers how to spray their trees. He then set up a cooperative through which the spraying could be done regularly
thereafter for about $1 an acre. Exports more than doubled
the first year, adding $60,000 in income. The next year,
they multiplied seven times over, and far more orders
were received than could be filled. The United Nations
was even able to persuade the shipping company which
took the fruit from Libya to southern Italy to cut its
freight charges in half. The whole industry began to come
alive.

THE UN HELPS GOVERN

Help in education and agriculture was just the beginning. United Nations people were invited into government offices to advise the responsible ministers on policy.
One UN economist himself served as director of the Development Council. Another was made adviser to the
national bank. An expert from Pakistan worked out proposed income tax legislation, which Parliament adopted
in substantially unchanged form. The International Labor Office helped draft a law to reform and strengthen
the social security system. An International Civil Aero-
nautics Administration (ICAO) man drew up a civil avi-
ation law which, together with other steps, enabled Libyan
airports to become important travel hubs in North Africa.

Libya had never taken an adequate census of its population. It needed one, not only to plan its economic development but to apportion seats properly in Parliament.
An Egyptian expert brought in by the United Nations
worked up a census plan and then directed its execution,
with more than one thousand Libyan civil servants per-
forming the house-to-house count.

Other statistics were urgently needed. The government set up a central statistical bureau and asked the UN to provide an expert to head it. The UN did so, finding such a man in Cyprus. He sat down with a staff of eight Libyans, whom he helped train, and began giving the country the statistical insights it needed. Here, too, as in other areas, the UN actually ran an important segment of the government.

Virtually every UN agency at one time or another had a hand in the task of lifting Libya by its bootstraps. The United States, Britain, France, Italy, Turkey, Egypt, and other countries pitched in with direct, bilateral aid programs, and with money to help pay for the UN aid. Several of these bilateral programs were larger in personnel and budget than the UN program; the American one was a lot larger. The Libyan government played an active and responsible role at the core of the whole operation.

Tragedy—and Counteraction

At first it was a slow and even discouraging task. There were setbacks. In 1957, the government distributed several hundred thousand fruit trees, free, in the coastal belt and the low mountain areas. But the farmers did not know how to care for the trees, and there were not enough trained people to tell them how. The land was poorly prepared, and orchard sites were not always selected carefully. No terraces were built on sloping sites; holes dug for many trees were too shallow. When the trees did take root, sheep and goats were often allowed to browse on them, injuring or killing them. The farmers did not value the trees very highly, since they had come from the government as a gift. In the first year, 90 per cent of the trees died.

It was a tragedy, but Libya did not waste time weeping. With the help of the UN, the government set out to correct the mistakes. In 1958, a British expert, Boyce Thrower, was brought in by FAO. Under his supervision, and that of the United States aid mission, 56,000 new trees —olives, almonds, apricots, plums, peaches, grapevines, figs, apples, pears, oranges, and limes—were sold, not given, to the farmers. They were carefully planted on selected sites under expert supervision. Months were spent training Libyans in the basic principles of caring for the trees. The farmers were offered bonuses if 85 per cent or more of the trees on their land survived.

The scheme worked so well that in 1960, the second year, 600,000 trees—more than ten times as many as in 1959—were planted. The greater majority of those plantings have survived. The tragedy of 1957 has been turned into a triumph.

All this, good as it was, was preamble. Libya came into its own with the discovery of oil in 1957.

The first gusher that shot up over the hot Sirte Desert meant a whole new future for the country. Whereas previously the desert had symbolized poverty, now it meant possible riches—especially if the wealth was properly used. Twenty possible drilling sites, not only of oil but also of natural gas, were found.

EXPLOITING THE NEW WEALTH

The UN played no significant role in this discovery; it was made by private companies, though in some cases preliminary UN surveys helped provide groundwork. But the UN, through pre-investment work, had helped prepare Libya to benefit from her good fortune. Now the UN stepped in to help exploit the discovery—to help Libya market the product, train the technicians needed, build related industries, and put the revenues to constructive long-range use. Largely at the UN's suggestion, the government decided to earmark 70 per cent of the revenues received by it for economic development. The government was determined that oil in Libya should not simply mean air-conditioned Cadillacs, palaces, and huge foreign bank balances for a chosen few.

It would be poetic justice if Libya, one of the poorest if not the poorest independent country in the world in 1952, should become, during the UN Development Decade, one of the countries with the most promise. To go from the first, elementary stage of development—from a traditional society—to the third, or "take-off" stage of development in less than twenty years would be an immense accomplishment. It would prove what free enterprise under government supervision can do, given outside help and some luck in the discovery of unknown physical resources.

Libya is a kind of microcosm of what the UN tries to do for a traditional society. There are, broadly, nine major contributions the UN makes:

1. It supplies international civil servants for temporary strengthening of the government—in some cases, men who actually run government departments; in others, advisers to aid the responsible cabinet minister.

2. It establishes and/or helps operate local institutes to

train people, at all levels, to run the government and other services themselves.

3. It strengthens the public school system, aiming at universal education as quickly as possible but putting special emphasis on teacher training and the development of skilled technicians for business, industry, and agriculture.

4. It helps to build up a better system of communications—roads, telephone, telegraph, radio, newspapers, books, and magazines.

5. It surveys the resources of the country, hoping for breakthroughs like the discovery of oil in Libya, but in any event desiring to put to best use whatever there is at hand—water power, minerals, rich unused land, etc.

6. It supplies experts in agriculture to advise on reforestation, crop rotation, seed selection, rural cooperatives, community development, rural extension services, crop diversification, and land reform where needed.

7. It provides experts to advise on the development of small-scale industries based on local arts and crafts, and to lay the basis for expansion of markets.

8. It encourages increased exports of cash crops, minerals, and other local products that will earn foreign exchange.

9. It helps lay the foundation for an effective tax system.

There are scores of countries in which this nine-point program, or a major portion of it, is being put into operation. Libya is only one example. Hundreds of millions of people in virtually every primitive country and territory in the world have felt the impact of the UN's extraordinary Operation Bootstrap.

12

THE INTERNATIONAL ASSAULT
ON POVERTY, 1950–1962

THE CONCEPT of helping whole nations improve
their lot through economic development—and of doing it
in one's own enlightened self-interest—is a product of our
generation. It proceeds directly from changed attitudes toward poverty and exploitation of resources at home.

Until recently, people in the United States were ex-
ploiting rivers and forests and "mining" land instead of
developing these resources. A relatively high percentage of
people were expected to live in poverty; that was the way
it had always been.

These attitudes have changed markedly. Headlong
exploitation of resources in the United States is now
generally regarded as short-sighted and self-defeating.
Widespread poverty—at least hopeless poverty of the type
that prevailed during the depression a quarter of a century ago—no longer is regarded as inevitable. It has virtually been wiped out.

These new attitudes on the part of the United States

and other industrialized countries found an early expression in the establishment of the International Bank for Reconstruction and Development (the World Bank) in 1944. They received vicariously a powerful stimulus in the spirit and method of the Marshall Plan. They were given further impetus by the launching of the United Nations Technical Assistance Program and the United States Point Four Program in 1949. Thereafter, programs of aid for the underdeveloped countries multiplied rapidly.

THE DIMENSIONS OF UNITED STATES AID

Between 1945 and 1960, United States government economic aid programs (exclusive of investment in international financial institutions) amounted to some $50 billion —a large sum, but one which represented less than two-thirds of 1 per cent of the United States' gross national product over the fifteen-year period. This $50 billion was by no means all aid to underdeveloped countries. More than half of it went to Western Europe (under the Marshall Plan and other programs), and another $2.5 billion went to Japan. Only $22.09 billion was allocated for assistance to economic development of poor countries, and much of this was "defense support," designed to subsidize cooperative allies. Military aid amounted to $27.84 billion and represented 34 per cent of American aid during the same period, even if "defense support" money is considered wholly "economic." The fact that military aid and economic aid have been generally lumped together as "foreign aid" has helped to distort the picture.

Most of the United States' aid money went directly to foreign governments; a comparatively small amount was channeled through the UN. Naturally, none of the mili-

tary aid (or related "defense support") went through the
UN. None of the aid to Western Europe did so. Of the $22
billion which can be classified as economic aid to underdeveloped countries, including Eastern Europe, only $1.5
billion or 7 per cent was channeled through international
organizations. The $22 billion compares with defense ex-
penditures totaling more than $500 billion and a gross
national product of $5,653 billion over the same fifteen-
year period, 1947–1961.

TABLE 2

UNITED STATES GOVERNMENT FOREIGN ASSISTANCE: CUMULATIVE
TOTAL, 1945–1960
(*billions of dollars*)

Military grants	$27.84
Defense-support grants (1951–1960)	9.30
Economic grants and credits (other than defense support)	40.64
Investment in international financial institutions	4.95
Grand total	$82.73

Distribution of economic grants and credits (including defense support):

Western Europe (excluding Greece and Turkey)	$25.32
Japan	2.53
Eastern Europe	1.44
Underdeveloped countries outside Eastern Europe	19.12
International organizations	1.53
Total economic aid	$49.94

SOURCE: Quarterly report, "Foreign Grants and Credits by the United
States Government," Office of Business Economics, Department of Commerce.

In addition to what the United States government has
done, private agencies were and are in the picture. Other

industrially advanced countries also have had important foreign aid programs.

INTERNATIONAL EFFORTS

The early 1950s saw the United Nations family begin to mobilize the assets at its disposal. These assets were, and are, considerable: a network of agencies, each with particular competence; a pipeline to a rich storehouse of skills and knowledge in many countries; a guarantee of political impartiality; and a sense of responsibility for the well-being of all nations.

The only resource that had to be added before the UN could launch its program was money. When sixty countries followed the United States' lead in 1950 and volunteered a starter fund, the *United Nations Expanded Program of Technical Assistance*—a worldwide idea-sharing enterprise—was born.

In the twelve years that have followed, the Technical Assistance Program has sent out some 11,000 experts, helped 20,000 students to be trained abroad, and participated in one way or another in the development of 150 countries and territories. It is teaching farmers in Thailand how to improve their rice crop by controlling the diseases that affect this crop; it is showing fishermen in Haiti that their catch and their sales can be multiplied many fold by the use of motorized boats and simple refrigerating units; it helped to rebuild a town in Liberia that had been completely destroyed by fire.

All this, and much more, has been done on a shoestring —a budget which began at $20 million and still today is only $43 million. The UN has never obtained from gov-

ernments more than a very small part of the total money
they were willing to spend on foreign aid.

The *United Nations Special Fund* for "pre-investment"
planning and action was established in 1959. As we have
seen, the Special Fund prepares the ground for fruitful
private and public investment.

In the first four years of its life (1959–1962) the Special
Fund approved 246 projects requested by seventy-one
countries and territories, either individually or in regional
groupings. It earmarked some $210 million—which has
been more than matched by the requesting countries.
Benefiting countries have put up $290 million—making
the ratio of government money to UN money nearly ten
to seven. The ratio shows the willingness of poorer countries to put their limited financial resources on the line for
an opportunity to receive United Nations aid.

The *International Bank for Reconstruction and Development* (the World Bank) is an affiliate of the UN. It
began with war reconstruction loans in the early postwar
years and then shifted to lending for development projects. By mid-1962, it had made more than three hundred
loans to sixty countries and territories involving total
commitments of more than $6.3 billion. Of this amount,
underdeveloped countries borrowed $3.917 billion.

In 1956–1957 another United Nations lending agency
was created: the *International Finance Corporation* (IFC).
Its commitments up to mid-1962 were relatively modest,
amounting to only $61 million, of which $40 million had
actually been lent. Another important new lending agency
is the *International Development Association* (IDA), set up
in 1960 as an adjunct of the World Bank. It has agreed to
make $202 million in interest-free "soft loans."

IDA's role clearly will be increasingly important in the years to come, since opportunities for "bankable" loans of the kind the World Bank makes are drying up, whereas the need for "soft loans" is still very great. Why this is so is discussed in Chapter 14.

13

THE LESSONS OF EXPERIENCE

Rᴇsᴜʟᴛs from aid in the 1950s were not spectacular when measured in terms of improved living standards. Although precise figures are not available, indications are that the average 1950 per capita income in the one hundred underdeveloped countries and territories we have been discussing was about $90. In 1959, it had grown to a bit over $100. Gross income grew at the rate of 3 per cent a year, but the addition of two hundred million people in the underdeveloped world produced a net growth per person of only about 1 per cent. That is the equivalent of saying that each person got a raise of about $1 a year, or 2 cents a week, during the decade—a dangerously slow improvement.

How can this record be improved during the 1960s?

One way is to avoid the mistakes that were made in the 1950s. No apologies are necessary for those mistakes; it was a decade of experimentation from which much can be learned.

THE LESSON OF APPROACH

One serious and pervasive mistake of the 1950s was to think of development assistance programs as charity or "giveaways." They were not. Development programs are investments in people and prosperity—and investments in peace and freedom as well. They benefit both the giver and the receiver.

If assistance to the less-developed countries is considered charity in the future, many nations will contribute nothing because the view is widely held that governments should not use tax money for philanthropic purposes. Further, help to the low-income countries on this basis lacks continuity; it tends to be spasmodic. Finally, if economic assistance is considered charity, the effect on the countries accepting it is devastating; it saps the self-reliance of both leaders and people. Paternalism has no place in relationships among sovereign nations.

Closely allied to the "charity" mistake has been continuance of the "donor country–recipient country" point of view. These terms were perfectly acceptable in describing international relief programs, but they outlived their usefulness when attention shifted from relief to recovery and then to development. As this change occurred, the relationship between the nations changed into a partnership—a partnership in an international joint venture to relieve human misery and expand the world economy.

To be sure, the industrially advanced nations are contributing much of the capital to the venture; but the contributions of energy, dedication and social transformation, as well as capital, by the underdeveloped countries represent much more difficult sacrifices and are equally vital to its success.

THE NEEDS OF THE RICH

An expanding world economy is as critically needed by industrially advanced nations as by underdeveloped ones. The richer countries are heavily dependent for their future well-being on the underdeveloped countries—for markets, materials, and an orderly world. What happens in the underdeveloped world will have a tremendous influence. The Congo has reminded us of that. In this titanic effort, all nations are donors and all nations are recipients.

The leaders of low-income countries, for their part, have in too many cases failed to recognize that no matter how much technical assistance, pre-investment help, and investment their countries receive from the outside, they and their people must bear the overwhelming share of responsibility for their own economic and social progress. External aid has only a limited, though vital, role. Theirs is the greater task; theirs is the greater sacrifice; theirs is the greater burden. The people of these countries must clearly understand that only they can bring about the better life they seek.

The other side of the picture, of course, is recognition by the industrially advanced countries that their role— though vital—is modest. They can help only people who are determined to help themselves.

The fact that external assistance has a vital but limited role to play was well demonstrated by the Marshall Plan. In 1949, the year of the most massive aid, $5 billion worth of American goods were sent from America to Europe. These goods represented 3 per cent of the gross national output of the European countries. Without them European recovery would have been more difficult, and their psychological impact was great; but 97 per cent of the tangible effort which produced that recovery was put in by the Europeans themselves. Well over 90 per cent of the effort required to bring about development of the modernizing countries today must be put forth by the people of the modernizing countries themselves.

PREJUDICE AGAINST PLANNING

International development programs suffered in the 1950s from an ill-defined but often deep-felt prejudice against anything that involved "planning." For many years, the concept of government planning was suspect domestically in the United States, and this attitude rubbed off onto international planning efforts.

Resistance to planning persisted despite the fact that every successful business plans its development and expenditure program as far ahead as possible; part of its resources are always allotted to development work—to a search for new products, to the expansion of markets. But paradoxically, what was considered good for business was considered bad for governments.

Fortunately, this mistake has been largely corrected. In the case of the modernizing countries, it is now recognized that physical and human resources must be used with as little lost motion and waste as possible. It is virtually criminal to throw money and energy away when both are in such short supply. Avoidance of waste demands an organized plan and carefully-thought-out programs to implement it.

One of the most damaging mistakes of the 1950s was a failure to realize that development cannot proceed without concentrating on an increase in human knowledge and skill. Despite our long traditions of veneration for individual man, we did not take into account his real significance in economic development. We failed to observe accurately enough. We looked at Switzerland and Japan, for instance, and did not see that human ingenuity, capacity, and skill had overcome tremendous handicaps of natural resources. It is a mistake no sensible observer will make again.

A further mistake has been to regard assistance to the less-developed nations as something temporary in nature, as an unpleasant task for which annual appropriations reluctantly had to be made. Development programs must be thought of not in terms of years but of decades. The year-by-year approach has been absurdly wasteful and inefficient.

Buying Friends and Allies

Still another serious mistake has been the failure of the industrialized nations to accept the task of speeding development of the low-income countries as an objective worthy of achievement for its own sake. Instead, foreign aid has been considered a tactical weapon in the cold war—a system of buying allies, winning friends, and influencing peoples.

As a result, many programs have been hastily conceived and badly executed. Much of the money has gone into projects that have had little effect on economic development. Some countries have received too much of the wrong kind of aid at the wrong time; others have received too little aid of any kind. The principals in the cold war have found themselves in the position of being played off against one another—of being virtually blackmailed into offering aid. The net result has been the waste of hundreds of millions, perhaps even billions of dollars. There has also been disillusionment when friends did not "stay bought."

A program for development of the underdeveloped areas would be necessary whether or not there was a cold war. Hunger would be disturbing in an amicable world, just as it is in a world of political turmoil. The demands of the ill-fed, ill-housed, and illiterate peoples of the world would still be great, and our obligations and self-interest to assist in meeting those demands would still be real, if political tranquility were the international rule.

What is needed is a recognition that speeding the development of the less-developed countries will help achieve a fundamental objective: the creation of economically self-sustaining nations independent of domination by the United States, the Soviet Union, or any other external power.

THE ADVANTAGES OF THE UN

In this connection, it has been a major mistake to overlook, as we have, the unique advantages of channeling aid through the United Nations and its specialized agencies. These bodies have accumulated the richest experience in virtually every field of development activity that can be found anywhere. The United Nations draws on the whole world for its technicians.

Further, United Nations assistance is a cooperative endeavor, with a voice for all countries regardless of their size or wealth, and with all countries contributing to the cost. Rich and poor are working together for the same goal: a progressing world. No country is so rich that it cannot benefit from an expanding world economy; no country is so poor it cannot contribute something.

The feeling of partnership has many happy by-products. It stimulates maximum self-help, cutting down on the cost to donors. It enables UN officials to "get tough" with recipient governments without stirring resentment, thus saving money and improving efficiency. It gives the UN a freedom to make demands which, were they made by one government upon another, would be regarded as hateful "strings." The recipients of help repeatedly declare their preference for aid given through the United Nations, since it is offered with no political, commercial, or military motives.

Developed countries often are direct beneficiaries of UN aid. Even the United States has received help. A Chinese expert advised Louisiana rice farmers on techniques for producing fish crops in their rice fields, thereby increasing the earning capacity of their farms.

Some years ago an African government which was attempting to compile its first census got an expert from a highly developed country to train its people in the use of "calculating machinery." When the expert arrived, he looked at an office full of machinery which was obsolete in his country before he was born. He shortly had a nervous breakdown.

Months later, the United Nations sent a statistician from a neighboring country. He was successful because similar problems had existed in his own experience. Furthermore, he spoke the language, was familiar with the equipment, and his approach was compatible with that of the country he was trying to help. With all the good will in the world, advanced countries are not always the best qualified to extend help.

The correct—indeed the only sound—approach to the channeling of aid is to select the channel which will give the most effective results at the lowest possible cost. This means using the UN much more frequently than we have in the past. The day has gone by when we can afford to see the slender resources available for development wasted in a futile attempt to buy friends, obtain commercial advantage, or get national credit.

It is apparent therefore that economic development programs are not charity; that all participating nations are both donors and recipients; that economic development is a goal worthy of being pursued for its own sake; that it can succeed only with those who help themselves; and that it can frequently be assisted more efficiently and less expensively through the United Nations.

Above all, development must proceed at a faster pace. That the 1950s taught us this transcendent lesson was dramatically demonstrated by the resolution of the United Nations General Assembly which invoked a Development Decade for the 1960–1970 period. There was not a single dissenting voice to this resolution, the unanimous view being that, of all the tasks before the people of the world, progress in the battle against misery was one of the most urgent. The following chart shows funds of UN and related agencies available for pre-investment and technical assistance programs.

CHART I

AGENCIES RELATED TO THE UNITED NATIONS WHICH PROVIDE INVESTMENT CAPITAL OR OTHER FINANCIAL ASSISTANCE

Agency or program	Resources	Activities
International Bank for Reconstruction and Development (World Bank)	Authorized capital $20,000,000,000	Loans to governments or with government guarantee for development projects
International Monetary Fund (IMF)	Members' quotas $15,000,000,000	Assists member governments through a pool of currencies available for short-term borrowing; promotes monetary stability; works against trade discrimination through monetary policy
International Finance Corporation (IFC)	Capital $94,000,000	Invests in private enterprise, mostly industrial, in association with private capital and management
International Development Association (IDA)	Authorized capitalization $1,000,000,000	Provides long-period loans to governments for development purposes, repayable on easier conditions than conventional loans

AGENCIES OF THE UNITED NATIONS WHICH PROVIDE TECHNICAL AND OTHER PRE-INVESTMENT ASSISTANCE

Agency or program	Funds available in 1962	Activities for Development
UN Special Fund	$60,000,000	Makes grants to governments for large-scale surveys of natural resources, for vocational and technical training, and for applied research institutes
Expanded Programme of Technical Assistance (EPTA)	($45,200,000, included in global resources of UN and other agencies below)	Provides experts and scientific fellowships and equipment for demonstration for projects handled by the UN and certain of its related agencies
United Nations Children's Fund (UNICEF)	$40,000,000	Aids development of national services in child health, nutrition, and maternal and child welfare; trains local personnel; provides equipment and materials needed from outside the country, including vaccines, insecticides, emergency food for children
UN Department of Economic and Social Affairs	$44,161,000	Helps in critical areas of economic development; e.g., industry and natural resources, public administration, social welfare, fiscal and financial services. Funds cover economic and social research and work on behalf of human rights, narcotics control, etc., as well as activities of regional economic commissions listed below. Also included is $850,000 for UN Operational, Executive, and Administrative Personnel (OPEX), to provide governments, on request, with senior officers to direct services or departments until national personnel can be trained adequately to take over

125

CHART I *(Continued)*

Agency or program	Funds available in 1962	Activities for Development
International Atomic Energy Agency (IAEA)	$ 7,024,925	Furnishes advisory services; surveys of future nuclear power needs; provision of equipment; fellowships in the field of peaceful uses of atomic energy
International Labour Organization (ILO)	$15,726,067	Provides advisers or instructors on labor problems and projects; training program includes exchanges of workers between countries
Food and Agriculture Organization (FAO)	$24,216,874	Supplies technical and scientific skills, some equipment; advisory services in agriculture, forestry, fisheries and nutrition; training and fellowships
United Nations Educational, Scientific and Cultural Organization (UNESCO)	$23,101,406	Supplies skills and advisory services in educational and scientific fields; fellowships and teaching personnel
World Health Organization (WHO)	$30,636,228	Makes available advisory services, skills and some equipment on medical and public-health programs including anti-malaria campaign; fellowships and training
International Civil Aviation Organization (ICAO)	$ 6,506,967	Supplies technicians, experts and advisory services in the field of civil aviation; training of personnel
International Telecommunication Union (ITU)	$ 4,071,491	Provides advisers and technical skills on projects in the communications field
World Meteorological Organization (WMO)	$ 1,336,044	Provides advisers and scientific skills on projects in meteorological field; training through fellowships

ARMS OF THE UNITED NATIONS INTEGRATED WITH TECHNICAL ASSISTANCE ACTIVITIES

Agency or program	Activities
Regional economic commissions for Europe (ECE); headquarters, Geneva, Switzerland Latin America (ECLA); headquarters, Santiago, Chile Asia and the Far East (ECAFE); headquarters, Bangkok, Thailand Africa (ECA); headquarters, Addis Ababa, Ethiopia	All maintain secretariats and assist governments on economic development plans and programs, with advisory services; preparation of statistical data and reports on the regional economy, or that of individual countries; and with conferences and seminars

126

United Nations—S. R. Weissenstein

At the entrance of the Nahal Shikma Watershed Pilot Project—the author (at left) with other representatives of the UN and officials of the Israeli government.

United Nations

The sixteenth session of the General Assembly unanimously declared the 1960s as the "United Nations De-

cade." added impetus to international economic cooperation.

14

GOALS FOR 1960–1970: A UN
DECADE OF DEVELOPMENT

THE United Nations General Assembly issued a call to the conscience of mankind when it labeled the decade of the 1960s a UN Decade of Development—a decade in which to make major inroads against hunger, poverty, ignorance, and disease.

The Assembly set as its goal a 5 per cent increase each year in the aggregate income of the developing countries. This may seem high, since in the 1950s the average yearly increase was only slightly over 3 per cent, but it is a necessary goal. The annual increase in population in the 1960s probably will be even higher than it was during the explosive 1950s, largely because of further decreases in the death rate. This means that a 5 per cent increase in a country's aggregate income will produce something less than 3 per cent net annual increase in income per person. It means a per capita increase over the ten-year period between 1960 and 1970 of less than $30—an increase from

$100 in 1960 to less than $130 in 1970 in the under-developed world.

Surely this is the very minimum at which we should aim. This goal probably will be exceeded by many countries; in fact, a number are already doing so—Brazil, Colombia, Greece, Mexico, Philippines, Puerto Rico, Taiwan, Turkey, and the Federation of Rhodesia and Nyasaland among them. Any lesser goal for the rest of the underdeveloped world would be utterly inadequate if mounting pressures of impatience and demand are to be released into constructive channels.

A staggering amount of foreign exchange will be required, however, if the modernizing countries are to reach this goal. They will need to import in the neighborhood of $440 billion-worth of goods and services, and will have to pay for it in foreign currency.

SOME EARNINGS FROM EXPORTS

How can imports of this magnitude be paid for? First, the less-developed nations will have foreign exchange earnings from the sale of their own goods abroad. Assuming the richer countries continue to need and buy these goods at the present, slowly growing rate, and assuming prices remain reasonably constant, I would estimate that the poorer countries will earn in this way roughly $378 billion of the $440 billion they need.

The less-developed countries would thus require some $62 billion in foreign exchange, over and above export earnings, to cover the estimated cost of import requirements. In addition, at least $8 billion would be needed to cover such other costs as debt service and transportation, bringing the total foreign exchange requirements up to $70 billion for the Development Decade.

This $70 billion is what I call "catalytic" capital. It is that portion of the total international flow of capital which is reserved strictly for development purposes.

In the first three years of the Development Decade, 1960–1962, the catalytic capital flow reached the sum of $14 billion ($4.25 billion in 1960, $4.75 billion in 1961, and about $5 billion—perhaps somewhat more—in 1962). Subtracting the $14 billion which has already been received from the $70 billion needed during the ten-year period leaves a balance of $56 billion which will be needed for 1963–1969 inclusive.

That means a flow of $8 billion over each of the next seven years. This is the crucial figure: $8 billion a year, each year until 1970, to enable poor countries to reach their minimum goals. Since the current annual catalytic capital flow is at the rate of something over $5 billion, nearly $3 billion per year not now in sight—roughly $21 billion in all—must be found.

Where will it come from? There is a good likelihood that $7 billion of this additional $21 billion will come through added private investment and through normal increases in so-called "hard" loans by governmental and inter-governmental institutions. That leaves $14 billion still to be found.

This $14 billion can be called "critical capital." It is essential to the transformation of our one hundred poor countries. It is the missing link in the chain upon which depends satisfactory progress during the remainder of the Development Decade.

Just what should this critical capital do? What is it needed for? How will it be managed?

THE PURPOSES FOR WHICH IT SHOULD BE INVESTED

We have allowed for a probable maximum increase in private investment. We also have assumed increases during the decade in "hard" or "bankable" loans by public agencies (that is, loans by the World Bank, the U.S. Development Loan Fund and kindred institutions) to finance specific, directly productive projects. The funds now flowing from these sources, and any conceivable increase in them, will still not equal the volume of investment needed for doubling the rate of per capita income growth. It seems apparent that most of the extra $14 billion will have to be "soft" loans—public money, provided by governments in the form of unusually long-term, low-interest—or no-interest—credits.

The most important unmet need in the underdeveloped countries is for this kind of loan, the kind that finances facilities and services which may not produce identifiable and recoverable revenues but which must exist if private capital is to be attracted into productive enterprise, or if public investment in production is to pay off.

I refer to schools, hospitals, and garbage collection services; telegraph, telephone, and postal networks; agricultural extension services; credit facilities; pilot housing; power development; irrigation; transportation—things which are needed but which do not always meet bank standards for directly assignable revenue production. These are essential furnishings of any economy, and without outside help in building them, a low-income country is condemned to decades, if not centuries, of slow and painful struggle with extreme poverty.

Here is a challenge to the more advanced countries: to

have the vision and confidence to make investments of this kind which are big enough (and have an assured continuity over a period long enough) to enable the developing countries to bring their economies to a point where they will be self-propelling.

In the Marshall Plan operations, we used a rather fancy word, "infrastructure"—which means "underpinnings" or "foundations." Investments in infrastructure provide the underpinnings of self-perpetuating economic advance. Only if we make adequate investments of this kind will we be sure of the increase in "bankable" loans which we assumed. If we do make such adequate investments, our estimate of the probable level of "bankable" loans may well be too low, even much too low.

The great bulk of the $14 billion of critical capital needed to fill the investment gap during the 1960s must, therefore, be investment in infrastructure. (A smaller portion must go into pre-investment activities such as resource surveys and training institutes.) These investments, as I suggested, must be exceptionally long-term loans, with exceptionally low interest rates, and in most instances they should provide for deferred interest and principal payments.

Loans of this kind are sometimes looked upon with condescension as "giveaways." While the phrase "soft loan" may be used as a convenient means of distinguishing non-bankable loans from bankable loans, I object to the implication that these would not be sound investments. This kind of financing would probably be the soundest investment the advanced countries could possibly make. Without this type of investment most other types would be jeopardized.

How It Should Be Managed

Such is the nature of the capital needed to fill our estimated gap of $14 billion. Now we can proceed to the second question: Through what managerial body is this capital to be applied and administered?

We have learned from experience in the 1950s that an international organization has tremendous advantages in dealing with underdeveloped countries, and it is through some multi-national or international organization that these "infrastructure" investments should be made.

From the United States' point of view, there is a special reason why reliance should be placed on an international method of operation. Under such an arrangement the United States would carry a smaller share of the burden. The countries of Western Europe, now fully recovered, are able to invest more in underdeveloped areas than they are now doing. Their gold and foreign exchange holdings, as well as their capacity to earn more, are increasing. The United States, on the other hand, is facing a continued deficit in its balance of payments, and its gold stocks are fluctuating. It is clearly in the United States' interest to spread the responsibility for investment in the underdeveloped areas and to induce other countries to make their maximum contribution. If the United States should declare itself and exert its influence in favor of extending the multilateral approach, the prospects would be greatly increased for full participation by other industrialized countries.

It is often suggested that new international studies of needs and capabilities are necessary as the basis for an additional or an expanded program of investment in the underdeveloped countries. I do not think any more general studies are needed. What is needed is action. But if studies for this are to be made, I suggest strongly that they should be made by the United Nations, for two principal reasons. In the first place, the United Nations is already a treasure house of economic data concerning both the less-developed and the industrialized countries. In the second place, it is of greatest importance that the less-developed countries participate from the beginning in any studies of this kind and in any institution that might be established to administer such programs. What the newly developing countries fear most of all is a revival of colonialism in any form; what they seek most of all is dignity. We want maximum effort on their part. Their cooperation should be enlisted from the very first in any undertaking as partners in a common enterprise.

In my view, at least half of the $14 billion in additional investment in the underdeveloped countries during the Development Decade should be channeled through the International Development Association, the new UN enterprise associated with the World Bank. This international lending agency is off to a good start, but its rate of lending—at $200 million a year—is well below the amount needed. IDA specializes in fifty-year interest-free loans for just the kind of projects we have been discussing. There is an urgent need for it to expand its operations rapidly, and I cannot see how the need for the IDA-type of loan can be met with anything less that $1 billion of investment per year.

Assuming that IDA is provided with $1 billion a year over a seven-year period, so that $7 billion in critical capital will be supplied, the remaining $7 billion will have to be provided by national development loan funds and regional funds such as the European Fund, with assistance from the United Nations. The UN should supply a substantial amount of the funds required for pre-investment activities.

If all this is done—but only if it is done—the Development Decade of the 1960s will begin to satisfy the hopes of millions. Only in this event will the modest goals which the General Assembly has proposed have a chance of realization.

15

THE PROMISE OF TOMORROW

THOUGH the decade of the 1960s is called the UN Development Decade, it would probably be more accurate to speak of it as the first UN Development Decade. The 1970s, 1980s, and 1990s will certainly see the struggle continuing.

But 1960–1970 is the crucial period. During these years, the patterns and foundations of development will be established. If man's innate dignity is to be recognized, if his right to determine his own political and social destiny is to have meaning, the remainder of this decade will be the time for the acceptance of these ideas.

The possibility of a major forward thrust in economic development is present. Science and technology are taking vast strides. Less than a quarter of a century ago space travel was a comic strip affair. Now the Soviet Union and the United States are racing to put a man on the moon. In large parts of the world UN teams are erasing the malaria that has been endemic during the entire memory of man. In the summer of 1961, Danish scientists first demonstrated the possibility of controlled fusion of hydrogen;

tomorrow the supply of cheap usable power may be un-limited.

The fact that the frontiers of knowledge are being pushed further up and further out does not, of itself, assure a better world. If this new knowledge is used destructively, it means annihilation; but if used constructively, the future is bright with promise.

Progress will not be smooth and even; there will surely be some setbacks, some unfortunate turnings. As the first visible signs of improvement appear, the hopes and demands of underprivileged peoples which today are generalized will become specific. No matter what progress is made, it will whet the appetite for more. Like most of the rest of us, they will expect too much too soon.

IRREGULAR PROGRESS

Development will surge forward in one nation, lag in another, and go into reverse in still another. Jealousy and international hostility may increase in some regions. Even within a single country, various sectors of the economy will progress at uneven rates. This in turn can lead to political upheaval.

As development proceeds, certain manufacturers in the industrially advanced nations will have to meet new and stiffer competition. The "great powers" will lose the control over poorer countries that they once exercised through the purse strings. They may find themselves outvoted in world forums. They will have to learn to survive rebuffs and setbacks without modifying their essential principles and without panic.

There may be waste. Fortunately, the experience of the late 1940s and the 1950s will stand us in good stead.

We now know how to reduce waste or stop it before it becomes aggravated. But an effort on the scale necessary for worldwide economic development cannot be made without the likelihood that some dollars, *cruzeiros, rupees,* and *rials* will go down the drain. To withhold participation in one of the most exciting and heartening enterprises of history simply because part of it might be wasted is like declining to start a fire because some of the heat will go up the chimney. There may be waste, but the waste will be insignificant when compared with the benefits.

There may be violence. Some of it may result from wars for independence, some from the struggles for power among rival leaders, some from deliberate incitement of the masses by those who see in turmoil, unrest, and desperation an opportunity to impose totalitarian rule.

But the upheaval will be worse—a lot worse—if there is no progress. Despite all the difficulties and frustrations that might result, this decade can be the decade in which momentum for a more prosperous, orderly, and creative world community is achieved.

THREE ESSENTIAL ATTITUDES

In addition to sound programs, adequate pre-investment activities, and investment, three other essentials must be recognized and acted upon. All have to do with the spirit in which the task is approached.

First, there is the spirit in the underdeveloped nations. Fortunately, most of the leaders are dedicated to the welfare of their people. They recognize that they must battle not only against poverty but against tyranny and privilege as well. They know that, given the intensity of effort required to speed development, only freedom can inspire the necessary determination and willingness to sacrifice. They know that the human spirit is a vital factor in the transition from dependence to a self-sustaining economy.

Without confusing development and recovery, we can still learn from the Marshall Plan the significance of mobilized human spirit. When the plan was originated to produce recovery of Western Europe to the industrial and agricultural production levels it had enjoyed in 1938, the cost was authoritatively estimated at more than $25 billion. Further study reduced the estimate to $17 billion. In fact, the Marshall Plan cost $13 billion—of which about $2 billion is in process of being repaid. Net total cost: $11 billion. The factor which was not taken into account in the original predictions was the human spirit. The people of Europe went to work with will, with determination, and with hope. In two years, the European economy had not merely reached its prewar levels; agricultural production was 20 per cent higher and industrial production was 40 per cent higher than in 1938.

Second is the spirit that the people of the industrially advanced countries manifest toward the less-developed countries. As Barbara Ward, Lady Jackson, puts it:*

. . . the need is to remove the work of world development from the subsidiary attention of the wealthy nations and to make it a central theme of their diplomacy, their international relationships, their philosophy of world order, their hopes for a future in which not only groups and nations but the human race itself can hope to make this small planet into a habitable home.

This means in practice that foreign aid, instead of being the last item to go into national budgets and the first to

* "New Perspective in Economic Development," background paper, Oxford Conference on Tensions in Development, p. 8.

come out, must be given high priority—second only to defense. Compared to the $120 billion scheduled for defense expenditure in 1962 by the member countries of the United Nations, $8 billion a year required to finance development adequately is not large. It will, in the long run, mitigate the need for future defense expenditures. It is past time that the national budget planners of the industrially advanced nations, and the politicians upon whom rests the responsibility for approving budgets in the democratic societies, recognize that the best and least expensive long-run defense of their national interests lies in the creation of a world in which poverty, deprivation, illiteracy, and disease are not constant provocations to violent and destructive upheaval.

The World Grows Smaller

Third, we must recognize that the world is indeed smaller. In 1961 Gherman Titov went around it seventeen and one-half times in just about one day. In 1962 John Glenn saw the sun rise and set three times in about four hours. Others followed. To make this world habitable, people must get rid of the limitations which their own narrow horizons impose on their view of the planet and its problems. As the underdeveloped nations emerge from industrial and material backwardness, their people and the people of the industrially advanced nations must jointly develop a new way of looking at themselves—a new vision clearly focused on the interests of all humanity. It has never been clearer in human history that all men are brothers; the economic facts of today's world point unfailingly at total interdependence. The social, spiritual, and political facts of life add emphasis which directs us—

for our own safety—to act as though all men are brothers whether we are willing to admit it or not. In this respect, the people of all nations are underdeveloped; they must struggle together toward mutual respect and a common dedication to common constructive goals.

If those industrially advanced nations to whom human dignity and freedom are underlying beliefs commit themselves as wholeheartedly to the effort for economic development as the peoples of the underdeveloped world are doing, the decade of the 1960s can provide two gigantic lasting benefits.

First, by 1970 perhaps twenty nations will have achieved self-sustaining economies. Mexico and Argentina can be two of them; India can be close on their heels. Each time an underdeveloped nation transforms itself into an industrially self-sustaining nation under free institutions, the cause of freedom achieves an incalculable victory. For, given the choice, people will always elect freedom. And there is no substitute for example. The struggling peoples of the entire world will look to their future with new hope if they can see clearly that their efforts, sacrifice, and dedication are going to pay off in spiraling spiritual, social, and material improvement.

Second, by 1970 major momentum—major impetus—for worldwide development can have been built up everywhere. Succeeding decades of development can follow the road maps charted in these next years.

By the year 2000, we can be living in a world that has overcome poverty—a world without want.

INDEX